INFINITE

The INFINITE WAY LETTERS 1958

By
Joel S. Goldsmith

DeVorss & Company, Publishers

ISBN: 0-87516-630-X

Originally published in 1959
Second DeVorss & Company printing, 1993

DeVorss & Company, Publisher
P.O. Box 550
Marina del Rey, CA 90294

Printed in the United States of America

CONTENTS

Except the Lord build the house, they
labour in vain that build it.
Psalm 127

Illumination dissolves all material ties and binds men together with the golden chains of spiritual understanding: it acknowledges only the leadership of the Christ; it has no ritual or rule but the divine, impersonal universal Love; no other worship than the inner Flame that is ever lit at the shrine of Spirit. This union is the free state of spiritual brotherhood. The only restraint is the discipline of Soul, therefore we know liberty without license; we are a united universe without physical limits; a divine service to God without ceremony or creed. The illumined walk without fear—by Grace.

From the book, *The Infinite Way*,
published by George Allen & Unwin Ltd.

Author's note: The portions of this book which are preceded by an asterisk (*) are spontaneous meditations which have come to the author during periods of uplifted consciousness and are not in any sense intended to be used as affirmations, denials, or formulas. They have been inserted in the book from time to time to serve as examples of the free flowing of the Spirit. As the reader practices meditation, he, too, in his exalted moments, will receive ever new and fresh inspiration as the outpouring of the Spirit.

CHAPTER ONE: JANUARY

SPIRITUAL UNFOLDMENT THROUGH THE STUDY OF THE INFINITE WAY

UNLESS spiritual teaching uses the letter of truth as a foundation upon which to build, it frequently results in a blind faith in some kind of a power outside of ourselves, a power that we expect and hope will do something for us. An understanding of spiritual principles is gained, first, by learning the letter of truth and, then, by applying it to the everyday problems of human existence—to our human relationships and to our headaches, corns, bunions, and simple colds. Eventually, we shall learn to apply these principles to the major problems of individual existence and finally come to the realization that these principles, if accepted, would operate in national and international affairs.

Merely as statements, truth is of no avail, but as we live with the letter of truth and continually abide in it, one day there comes a transitional experience. The mind is no longer repeating words, but words are coming to our awareness from within. The Bible, the writings of The Infinite Way, the tape recordings, the tape recording meetings, and the class work, if properly utilized, serve a twofold purpose. First, these implant the letter of truth in the mind and then they become the instruments by which truth becomes conscious awareness, a feeling in the heart.

In the early stages of the development of spiritual consciousness, you fill yourself with truth by reading, by listening to recordings and attending tape recording meetings, by individual study with a teacher who had gone a step beyond you, and by attendance at classes. The more inspirational literature you read, the more classes you attend, and the more recordings you hear, the more does your thought become spiritualized, and the clearer transparency for truth do you become.

Regardless of what path you may be following, you will find that there are certain disciplines to be observed: there is work to be done; there are periods when it is necessary to lift yourself into an atmosphere of God, to raise yourself up from the level to which you may have dropped because of the hypnotism of the world. To do that sometimes takes a considerable amount of study, meditation, and association with those on the path. There must be an actual knowledge of what the truth is, making it so much a part of your being that there is no possibility of your forgetting it in time of trouble. Let me illustrate that with the following quotation:

> *Our consciousness is the substance of our world. . . . We see the Infinite Invisible as the law, cause, and activity of all that is and drop concern for the form whether it be person, thing, or condition.*[1]

A hundred times a day that statement is contra-

[1] By the author. *Practicing The Presence* (New York: Harper & Brothers, 1958), pp. 17, 18, and (London: L. N. Fowler & Co. Ltd., 1956).

dicted. A hundred times a day you are reminded that you need money, you need clothes, you need food, or you must find safety and security. A hundred times a day arguments are presented contradicting the basic fact that your consciousness is the secret place of the most High, that that consciousness is your security and safety, and that there is nothing outside of you that can enter that consciousness to defile or make a lie. Your consciousness is the fortress and the rock, and because you are abiding there, nothing out in the world can enter that consciousness or your experience to injure, mislead, or deprive you of anything in life. A thousand times the suggestions of the world will be hurled at you, and each time your response must be, "No, safety and security are not found outside. Safety and security are found only in the secret place of the most High, in the temple of God within my own being, within my own consciousness."

It sounds very foolish to the human mind to be told that this consciousness which you are is a protection from germs and bombs. Yet that is the truth of Scripture. When Hezekiah urged his people who were confronted with a formidable army to take heart, "Be strong and courageous, be not afraid nor dismayed for the king of Assyria, nor for all the multitude that is with him: for there be more with us than with him: With him is an arm of flesh; but with us is the Lord our God to help us," you will find that "the people rested themselves upon the words of Hezekiah."[1] That is a strange reliance, is it not? You would think that they would have rested

[1] II Chronicles 32:7, 8.

in his army and ammunition; but no, they rested in the words of Hezekiah. We, also, are taught to rest—to rest in the word of Scripture.

When confronted with any form of error, it is often wise to ponder this passage of Scripture: "My glory will I not give to another."[1] God does not give Its power, substance, law, or activity to any form of sin, disease, or limitation. Think of the tremendous meaning here: No form of discord has power, activity, or law. No mortal concept, belief, or theory is spiritually endowed. No wonder Hezekiah said that they have only the arm of flesh, and then his people rested in his words. What faith and confidence! What power! "The people rested themselves upon the words of Hezekiah." Can we not likewise rest in the assurance that the armies of the enemy—all forms of error—are not spiritually endowed? God has not given Its power to them: They have only the arm of flesh, nothingness.

However, even after you have heard this and even after you believe it, it will only be a few hours before you will be tempted to disbelieve it or mistrust it—just long enough to hear a radio broadcast or read a newspaper headline. Then all of the truth is forgotten unless you are alert and have been willing to discipline yourself through study and by practice, so that you are instant in answering every suggestion and every appearance of evil with a conscious rebuke.

In your present state of development, it is necessary to recognize that every bit of evil presented to you in the world is suggestion or appearance. It may

[1] Isaiah 42:8.

well be that, because of the press of circumstances, you may be unable to stand fast in not accepting it into consciousness as a reality. In such situations, you would be wise to turn within and remind yourself of some truth:

> * What is this that is coming to me? Do I have to believe it? Why should I believe anything apart from God? God made all that was made, and all that God made was good. Anything God did not make was not made, and so this that is coming to me was never made. It has no reality; it has no substance, law, cause, or effect; and therefore, I do not have to believe it or accept it into my consciousness.

That is treatment. All you have done is to clear your own consciousness so that you do not accept the appearance as reality. Then you must become very still, "Speak, Lord; for thy servant heareth,"[1] and in that listening attitude make your conscious contact with God. Only when consciousness is opened to God is God made available.

Until you become convinced that the only power there is, is within your own being, you will be under the necessity of mentally disciplining yourself every time you come up against an appearance. Thus you will be building spiritual consciousness. Spiritual consciousness is your consciousness when there is a complete confidence in the Infinite Invisible.

The Bible

There is no better way to begin the development

[1] I Samuel 3:9.

of spiritual consciousness than with a study of the Bible. The Bible is a great historical document and, as a piece of literature, it ranks among the greatest because of its beauty of expression. It is not for such reasons that we read it, however, because for us, the Bible embodies a great spiritual teaching; it is a guide which can lead us in the way everlasting. We may find the historical and literary aspects of the Bible interesting, but our real interest is in the Bible as a way of life.

Infinite Way students should learn to carry a Bible with them wherever they go. Let it be a very thin Bible, which fits into the purse or bag, but always have a Bible close at hand, because God speaks to us principally through the Bible. You will be surprised to discover how comforting it is to receive an impulse from within, even a little push in the back, demanding, "Open that Bible and see what happens."

You can turn to many passages of Hebrew Scripture and find great truths in them, but you can take all the passages of the Master's unfoldment, accept them as literal truth, and go out and prove them. Buy a red letter edition of the New Testament and read in those red letters the words of the Master, but be sure that you do not take a sentence out of its context and thus cloud its meaning.

The Bible as a book will not reveal God to you. God was revealed to those who received the Word which became the Bible, and if you are faithful in your study of the Bible, you may receive enough inspiration so that you, too, can become receptive to God. The Bible is the fountainhead of spiritual wisdom and power, but Scripture merely read, memorized, or repeated is not spiritual power. Scripture must be spiritually discerned and then, and only then, does it become the power that brings peace on earth.

The Infinite Way

As I have watched the work of The Infinite Way unfold, it has seemed strange to me that so little actual study is given to the textbook, *The Infinite Way*. True, it is read, and occasionally, students go back to it and do further reading in it, but I doubt that there are many students who realize its full significance. *The Infinite Way*, small as it is, contains everything that we know up to this moment on the subject of spiritual unfoldment, spiritual living, and spiritual healing. In fact, practically every paragraph in this entire book is a metaphysical and spiritual text upon which a whole book could be written, and upon which many have already been written. There is not a single statement of truth in all our other writings that was not originally set forth in this one book. Hundreds of pages of additional material have been printed, but these ten, twenty-five, or fifty thousand word books may be only an amplification of one sentence found in *The Infinite Way*.

There is one short sentence in *The Infinite Way* that states that "anything that exists in the realm of effect is not cause, is not creative, and has no power over us."[1] That sentence alone would bear three year's earnest study. There is not a single

[1] By the author. *The Infinite Way* (San Gabriel, Calif.: Willing Publishing Company, 1956), p. 144.

discord within range of your thought that is not based on the belief that you are an effect and that there is a cause somewhere that can do something to you or for you.

The chapter on "Metaphysical Healing" states, "Healings are always in proportion to our understanding of the truth about God, man, idea, body."[1] I do not know how any serious student could spend less than a year dwelling upon that one sentence. He should write it out, put it up on the mirror, carry a copy in his pocket, and then, regardless of what he is reading for the next year, see what relation it has to God, man, idea, and body. If you knew the truth about God and man, the truth about idea and body would quickly reveal itself, because no one will ever find his freedom until he knows that he is not man. As long as the belief exists, consciously, unconsciously, or sub-consciously within you, that you are man, you will be seeking a God some place outside of yourself, and God cannot be found there. Ponder this statement on God, man, idea, and body until its inner meaning is revealed to you.

By dwelling on truth in this way, taking only one statement at a time and abiding in it, its *inner meaning* is made clear and the entire truth about it is revealed. Many passages of *The Infinite Way* will reveal important principles of living and healing if you will but study them, meditate upon them, and then *put them into practice in daily living*.

In practically every one of The Infinite Way books, you will find chapters on God, Soul, Spirit, or some of the other synonyms for God. Read all that

[1] *Ibid.*, p. 114.

you can find about a particular subject. For example, take the word God and read every chapter in the writings which deals with that particular subject. Study them thoroughly and meditate upon what you find. Leave all the other chapters of the book alone for the time being. Live with the word God for weeks or months at a time until an inner unfoldment of its real meaning is given to you. Then continue your study by taking up the synonyms for God in the same way. From them you may go on to such topics as "The Christ," "Prayer," "Meditation," "Communion," "Treatment," "Oneness," or "The Nature of Error." The order in which these subjects are studied is unimportant. What is important is that you are dwelling in some one facet of God or working with a specific principle of The Infinite Way until you have received a measure of illumination on it and are beginning to show it forth in your daily life.

The Wisdoms of The Infinite Way

The Wisdoms found in *The Infinite Way* came to me over a period of two years. Some students may not understand these Wisdoms because they are not man's wisdom: God gave them to me, and spiritual wisdom is requisite for an understanding of them. Before they were given out to the public, I released them to a small group of students for study and absorption into consciousness.

The first statement in The Wisdoms is:

> Begin your spiritual life with the understanding that all conflicts must be settled within your consciousness.

> There is never a conflict with person or condition . . .[1]

Could anything be more contradictory to everything that is happening in human experience? Human experience is a perpetual conflict with people and conditions. Spiritually that can never be true, however, because whenever there is a conflict within you, it is not a conflict with a person, even if some person seems to be involved. It is a conflict within you regarding your concept of the person or your concept of your relationship to him. Therefore, there is no call upon you to correct a person, to change him, or to reform him. The call is on you to go within yourself and re-establish the truth *about* the person. Then there is no further conflict, and you are in agreement.

In just the same way, there is no conflict with a sin, a cough, or with disease of any nature. To your sense of things, there may be a conflict because there seems to be something or somebody out in the world that you would like to eliminate from your experience. Whatever appears to be erroneous is but a false concept which you are entertaining and, therefore, there is nothing to be achieved by fighting a cough, a cancer, or polio, or for that matter, there is no use in fighting sin or even tyrants. Every conflict must be settled within your own consciousness. When you have resolved it there, you have yet to wait for that inner click, that deep breath, the release that assures you that God is on the field. Then when you turn your attention to that which

[1] *Ibid.*, p. 156.

has been causing the conflict, you will find that it is no longer there, and in its place is peace. You have not gone to God and asked Him to do anything about a person, a body, a sickness, a sin, or a lack. All you have done is to establish yourself in the correct letter of truth and wait for God's presence to be revealed.

> Therefore, make the correction within yourself, rather than attempt to change anyone or anything in the without.[1]

This is an important point in the healing work. You may be called upon for help once a day or a hundred times a day, but neither in the first nor in the one hundredth time should you try to change your patient. Some systems of metaphysics teach that certain traits of character cause disease, but to us a false trait of character is just as much of an error as the disease that it is supposed to have caused—and it is just as much of an illusion. To attempt to get rid of the trait of character would be working on the same level as would be the attempt to get rid of the disease itself. What you have to do is to turn, not only from the disease, but from the mental trait which is supposed to have caused it, and anchor yourself in the realization that God is the only cause.

Humanly, you are under the domination of thoughts; humanly, you are subject to thought. If you enter a room filled with kindly, generous, and loving people, you will feel the uplift of their thoughts and vice versa. We are all influenced by

[1] *Ibid.*, p. 156.

thought, but in The Infinite Way we have to learn not to react to thoughts, and the method of achieving that goal is given in The Wisdoms:

> When living out from the center of Being, you are untouched by the thoughts, opinions, laws, and theories of the world. Nothing acts upon you since you do not react to the world of appearances.[1]

This is not true, however, until you specifically lift yourself above the domination of human laws, opinions, and theories, and become attuned to the Spirit. Notice that nothing acts upon you *when* you do not react to the world of appearances. If someone should call you a thief, you would probably smile at such nonsense and go on your way, untouched and unhurt. If you are living in tune with God, you will not react to such an unfounded and untrue statement, you will not be insulted. You could only be insulted if it were true.

On the other hand, if someone should say to you, "I think that you are coming down with the 'flu'," you might immediately react with, "I wonder what I could have done to bring that on. Was I out in a draft yesterday?" But if you are in tune with the Spirit, your response will be of an entirely different nature, such as, "Nonsense, you may be subject to such a belief, but there is no truth in it at all. I am subject not to 'flu,' but to divine in*flu*ence, the in*flu*ence of God."

Success in meeting erroneous conditions lies in our reaction to them. A call may come that a patient is

[1] *Ibid.*, p. 157.

dying. That is the very time to practice the lesson of reaction: "Who convinceth me of death? The Master said, 'Which of you convinceth me of sin?'[1] And who convinceth me of death? Who is there that can make me react to the belief in a life apart from God?" You are a student of spiritual wisdom and you are called, not for the purpose of changing bad matter into good matter, or poor matter into rich matter, or sinful people into pure people, but for the purpose of establishing the Christhood of an individual.

> In the spiritual life, you place no labels on the world. You do not judge as to good or evil, sick or well, rich or poor. While appearances may show forth harmony and discord, by not judging you merely know IS, and let that which truly IS define Itself.[2]

By looking at someone, you cannot know whether he is sick or well because nobody can judge from appearances. The person you are seeing may look well, but that does not make it so. In fact, you do not even know if he is good or bad, rich or poor, high or low. There is only one thing which you do know about him: You know that he exists; you know that he is, and that is enough for you to know. Because God is infinite, there can be nothing to him but God since there cannot be a God *and* a he.

> To live spiritually is to know that all is, then do not name, label, define, or judge what is. Be

[1] John 8:46. [2] By the author. *The Infinite Way*, p. 157.

> content to know IS, and *let* what IS reveal Its being, nature and character to you.[1]

Someone may be presenting you with the appearance of either health or sickness, youth or age, life or death, but you must sit quietly until you come to this recognition of IS and then wait. You must know not only IS, but *who* is, *what* is, and *why* is, and what *eternally* is. Then the words may come, "This is my beloved Son, in whom I am well pleased."[2]

> Never seek anything or any condition in prayer. *Let* harmony define and reveal itself. Let your prayer be *letting* the IS appear.[3]

That is the exact opposite of the commonly accepted attitude toward prayer. If you want to pray for someone, let the Spirit reveal to you, "Thou art my beloved son, the chosen of God."

> Be sure that your prayer is not a desire to improve God's universe.[4]

If you took that one sentence out of *The Infinite Way* and lived with it for a month, so that every time you sat down to pray and the temptation came that your patient or student was unemployed, you would stand in your spiritual integrity and refuse to ask God to do anything about it. If you did nothing more than that until you settled back in peace and *let* God appear, you would be giving the most perfect

[1] *Ibid.*, pp. 157, 158. [2] Matthew 3:17.
[3] *Op. cit.*, p. 158. [4] *Ibid.*, p. 159.

treatment in the world and you would find that there would be no unemployment or discordant situation of any nature.

Abandon the hope that you are going to meet with a great power that is going to do something for you. God is a state of being, an *IS*ness which cannot be influenced to do any good for you. God is good; God is love; God is intelligence; God is omnipresent; and God is omnipotent. Your praying does not change that. It will not make it more so, nor will it make it effective in your case. It is always in operation, and all you can do is to bring yourself into attunement with It. The whole secret lies in learning to be attuned, and then you will find that the fullness of God is already within you.

Study The Wisdoms earnestly. Live with them day in and day out. Meditate on them and they will open up a way before you—the way of fulfillment.

The Recordings

Soon after the message of The Infinite Way reached the public through the writings, the call came for personal instruction, and that in turn led to the use of tape recordings. Through some electronic process, these recordings catch not only the words of the message, but actually the consciousness of the speaker. They convey to the hearer much more than the words themselves; they actually convey the spirit of the message. The writings and recordings are the means of preserving for us the wisdom that has been given to us. Through the tape recorder it is possible to hear the same message over and over again until the points which are important to individual unfoldment have registered in consciousness. The purpose of the letter of truth, whether presented in the writings or in the tape recordings, is not to develop the mind, but is really to serve in such a way that the mind becomes quiet and the Soul takes over. The hearing of the Word helps to build up in your consciousness an awareness of one Presence and one Power. Being thus reminded of God as the reality of being, once, twice, or three times a day or week, will eventually awaken you to the realization of God and the experience of greater harmony.

There are several hundreds of places in various parts of the world where this message is being heard by tape recordings in groups of from two, three, or five, up to groups of fifty, sixty, or seventy at a time. Classes that have been given in Australia can be heard in Seattle, Chicago, or London, and classes in Seattle, Chicago, or London can be heard in Australia. Wherever a class takes place, Infinite Way students all over the world have the opportunity of going through that same class. Instead of a group of 100, 200, or 500 people hearing the message, it can be heard, through the tape recordings, by thousands of Infinite Way students and their families, guests, or friends. Classes held all over the world during the last five years are available to students on tape. Attendance at group meetings during which these tape recordings are played will be helpful in providing the spiritual atmosphere which lifts consciousness and makes it receptive to the word of truth. "For where two or three are gathered together in my name, there am I in the midst of them."[1]

There is a spiritual bond uniting us. Throughout the twenty-four hours of every day, Infinite Way students are meeting somewhere in meditation, in prayer, and in contemplation. They are meeting to listen to the message as it is presented through the recordings and they will be in specific prayer and meditation for those of us who are united with them. These recordings serve as a bond between us, holding us in the one spiritual consciousness of the truth. Never are we apart from the spiritual activity of prayer; never are we without the benefit of the prayers of somebody, somewhere—of their communion and meditation in our behalf as well as in the behalf of the entire world. That is the purpose of this work.

Class Work

One of the most sacred experiences that can come into our lives, outside of the actual realization of God, is our class work. It is a sacred experience because it is the pathway that can lead us to the door of heaven. The kingdom of heaven itself, however, comes to us only as an activity of our own consciousness.

The value of a class cannot be measured from the standpoint of money. If a class were rightly appreciated, there would not be enough money to pay for one. The tuition for Infinite Way classes is comparatively low, not because their value is not recognized, but in order to make them available to

[1] Matthew 18:20.

those who are serious in wanting to walk this path and to make them available, not merely once or twice, but many, many times until the student comes to the place where he finds that he has made his contact with God—until he is consciously one with God.

Infinite Way classes are closed classes: A student who enrolls in these classes must be sufficiently familiar with the writings of The Infinite Way to have decided in his own mind whether or not this is the message that he desires and earnestly wants. Furthermore, he must have so arranged his activities and time as to be able to devote six consecutive days or evenings to attendance at the class sessions. Frequently, students who enroll in an Infinite Way class represent varied metaphysical backgrounds and at first are not completely one in their understanding of this message. By the second or third class session, however, they are gaining a greater understanding of The Infinite Way and are therefore coming closer and closer into agreement. There is a united consciousness open to the impartation of the Spirit, Itself. If I were to spend the entire hour or two in silence, the class would be successful because we would be so attuned to the one infinite Wisdom that we would receive divine impartations. Something more important is taking place than anything that is said from the platform, and whatever is said is immediately understood, received, and responded to in that one united consciousness.

My lifework is dedicated to bringing those who come into The Infinite Way to that place of consciousness where they themselves receive divine impartations and are no longer dependent upon books, teachers, or even classes. It is my hope that our work will produce students who are able to lift up consciousness to the point of conscious oneness with God. Any earnest student who comes to me or to anyone of uplifted consciousness for help and who comes regularly over a period of time can be so lifted that he comes to a place where he himself is receiving the impartation of the Spirit. That is the goal of The Infinite Way.

A closed class is an experience, not a teaching. If a closed class were something that could be given out of memory or from past experience or as a prepared paper carefully planned and outlined in advance, there could be a closed class every day of the week. But a closed class is not for the purpose of telling you what I have learned in the past forty years, nor of giving you a résumé and repetition of some intellectually perceived statements of truth. A closed class is an opportunity, after weeks and months of meditation and communion, for sufficient silence so that God may give us a message that is new and fresh today.

There is little which can be taught about God, but God can reveal Itself infinitely every moment to all of us. As I sit in a closed class, through my preparation of hours upon hours and days upon days of meditation, my consciousness has been opened to the revelation of God in me; and the students who partake of the class, through their preparation and through the work that has been done by them and for them, come with their consciousness open, not to hear a man but rather that God may reveal Itself in their consciousness. Strangely enough, that may come through me and through the things that are said through me, but not necessarily. It may come through an individual idea or thought that will present itself to the consciousness of the student while he is in the classroom, and may have nothing to do with what I am saying, or it may come when he reaches home after the meeting or in the middle of the night. It may even come two weeks or two months from the time the class was held, but when it comes it will be the revelation of God within. A closed class is an experience, and you will find that it is an experience of God in you. In coming into the closed class work, you are a part of a united spiritual consciousness which encircles the globe.

From the Letter to the Spirit

Young students must learn the letter of truth, and those who have gone through that basic discipline will have to maintain themselves in it. The correct letter of truth, in the measure in which we know it, leads to further unfoldments of truth. There are a few fundamental truths which constitute the letter of truth, and these must never be forgotten because of their basic nature and because of the effect that they have on our lives. But always remember that the light on these few truths must be individual and must be continuously flowing, new and fresh every day.

Attending classes, studying the writings, and hearing recordings which deal with the nature of God, the nature of individual being, the nature of the Christ, and the nature of error help to keep your temple clean. If you do not keep yourself immersed in Spirit by hearing and studying the Word, you may find yourself accepting the mesmerism of the world. Do not, however, be discouraged if you do not immediately comprehend the full and complete letter of truth sufficiently to be able to prove it in every experience of your daily life. It takes years to develop spiritual consciousness; it cannot be done in a few days or months.

Important as the letter of truth is, it of itself is of no avail: "It is the spirit that quickeneth,"[1] and the Spirit comes to us through our hours of meditation during which the letter is illumined. Then it becomes the meat, the wine, and the water—life itself. It is no longer in the realm of the mind, but has found a resting place in the heart. Accept the responsibility that is placed upon your shoulders.

> Meditate upon these things; give thyself wholly to them; that thy profiting may appear to all.[2] . . . Behold, I have set before thee an open door.[3]

ACROSS THE DESK

Look to this Day!
For it is Life, the very Life of Life.
In its brief course lie all the Verities and Realities of
your Existence:
The Bliss of Growth,
The Glory of Action,
The Splendor of Beauty.
For Yesterday is but a Dream,
And To-morrow is only a Vision;

[1] John 6:63. [2] I Timothy 4:15. [3] Revelation 3:8.

But To-day well-lived makes every Yesterday a
Dream of Happiness,
And every To-morrow a Vision of Hope.
Look well therefore to this Day!
—"The Salutation of the Dawn," from the Sanskrit

At this dawn of the New Year, I salute you with my love and my greetings!

Elbert Hubbard has given us a high concept of successful living when he writes, "The love you liberate in your work is the love you keep." I marvel that such deep wisdom can be found in such a short message.

Usually our lives are lived doing things that are given us to do, without consideration for the fact that there is something we would love to do or long to do. Perhaps it has been so many years since you have thought of what you would love to do that you either cannot remember what it was or else you feel that it is too late to begin it now.

Away with such thoughts! Turn within and ask yourself what you would like most of all to do. What is it that you long to put your heart and soul into achieving? What would you gladly devote your time, effort, and money to accomplishing? What could you do that would really bring true satisfaction: Is there some study you have always wanted to pursue? The great libraries can supply you with every book that is necessary. Is there a collection you would enjoy making—stamps, coins, rare prints, or books? Is there a worthy cause to further—Boy Scouts, Girl Scouts, Y.M.C.A. or Y.W.C.A.? Have you dreamed of developing skill in swimming, golf, or archery? Is there some subject which you found particularly interesting in school, but never had the time for its study?

First of all, search yourself this minute to find something to which you can devote your love, energy, and even your dollars. Regardless of how impossible the attainment or fulfillment of your goal may seem, acknowledge that there is this into which you would like to throw your whole self. This step must be taken—the acknowledgment that this is the one thing to which you can wholeheartedly give yourself, your entire self.

Fill yourself today with love for that old dream. Let yourself be thrilled with the love you once felt for your hopes. Let love fill your whole being with wonder at this resurrection of the vision which you have permitted to be buried these many years.

The next step is to take a few minutes every day to be alone with your dream. Can you perceive what can be accomplished—the joy you can give or receive, the service you might render, and all the good which may result? Think of the inner joy and satisfaction you can attain through that which you love so deeply. Think of the many empty hours which will be filled with happiness and peace through the higher consciousness in which you will live when your whole nature is changed by the love you devote to this that you so long to do.

Here is a secret I have learned "the hard way": Our problems cannot be permanently solved except by love—not the love others give us, but the love which flows out from us; and the most powerful love there is, the one which will wipe out all problems for us, is the love we put into the fulfilling of our dream.

Follow these first two steps and then watch for the unfoldment of the third step—that which will make possible your dream. You need only concern yourself with the first two steps; the third will come of itself. Find something to love—not someone. Then give yourself to it.

CHAPTER TWO: FEBRUARY

PROBLEMS AREN'T PROBLEMS ANY MORE

EVERY one of us has encountered problems of one nature or another. Most of us come to the study of spiritual wisdom because of some problem—physical, mental, moral, financial, or even something which may not fall into any of these categories. One of the most difficult of all problems, because it is so intangible and therefore so frustrating, is a sense of incompleteness; but this very sense of incompleteness is what forces us into a seeking for truth and spurs us on in our search for God. During the early stages of our unfoldment, problems really are problems, but if we are seriously following the spiritual path, we eventually come to a place where problems are no longer problems.

There are three stages in our experience with problems. The first period is when we have a problem that to us is a very real one, and we turn to a practitioner, teacher, or teaching for help in solving that problem. The practitioner with real spiritual discernment, however, will be able to point out, "Yes, it is true; you do have a problem, but your problem isn't what you think it is. Your problem really is a sense of separation from God; your problem is that you have not yet attained God-realization—not even a touch of it. You will find that when you attain a measure of God-realization, your problem will begin to fall away and eventually it will disappear." This does not mean that the first time we have a flicker of light, automatically, all our problems are going to be solved, but it means that in proportion as we attain God-consciousness our problems will begin to dissolve, and eventually, the nature of the problems will change.

The second stage of our unfoldment is that stage in which a problem becomes an opportunity, but it is only when we have come to this second stage that we can see a problem in that light. If we used such language with a beginner, he would probably reply, "I'd be glad to let someone else enjoy this glorious opportunity."

Many times students rail against problems, and yet no spiritual development at all would be possible but for problems. True, we would probably continue reading or attending classes and lectures, but we would not continue to progress spiritually because spiritual development comes through the practice of spiritual wisdom. It comes in much the same manner as success does in any field of work. For example, an accountant becomes successful because of applying his knowledge of bookkeeping to the many sets of books with which he has worked; an architect becomes successful only because of the many problems he has met in designing buildings. While people are engaged in surmounting their problems, they may not feel that they are meeting with any degree of success in life. It is only after a sufficient number of problems have been solved that the years of their success come, and then the right answer to any problem which may arise is always available.

So it is with us. We believe that we are so interested in God that nothing will ever interfere with or block our search for God, but it is surprising how many things can stop us. It is so easy to rest back in the comfort which may be found in being healthy, wealthy, or wise—in fact, health and affluence can be more of a problem than their absence. And so we come to a second stage of unfoldment in which problems are not problems any more: They have now become our opportunities. Jacob had reached that stage when he wrestled with the angel all night long and would not let him go: "I will not let thee go, except thou bless me."[1] It is when we are at that point that we, too, can say, "I don't want this problem to pass until I have seen the spiritual light that dissolves it, and which, in dissolving this problem, will dissolve all the problems which may be developing tomorrow or next year." In our human experience it is necessary for us to have some challenge which will arouse us and awaken us to our spiritual opportunities until, through persistence and perseverance, we come to God-realization.

Temporary harmony can be brought into your experience, and into the experience of your family and associates, through the uplifted spiritual consciousness of a practitioner or teacher, but that temporary sense of harmony does not constitute your life demonstration. Any healing that you may have or any improvement in your life which you may experience through the work of a practitioner or teacher must be gratefully accepted as a proof of

[1] Genesis 32:26.

the principle; but in the last analysis, it is you, yourself, who, through an activity in your own consciousness, must bear witness to the Christ in your life and in your work. Bear witness to the Infinite Invisible as the source, the law, the cause, and the allness of that which is visible; and bear witness that all the discords on earth represent only the activity of a universal belief in a selfhood, life, and law apart from God. Then you will be living by a principle and not by a person.

This leads to a place in consciousness where there is no judgment, no criticism, and no condemnation. It is a state of pure spiritual being in which we hold no one in praise or condemnation: We see through every appearance, recognizing it as only a snare and a delusion unto our feet. We recognize in each other but another form of the Christ, another individualization of God. There is not condemnation and there is not praise, but there is a recognition that there are states and stages of consciousness and that some individuals are farther advanced on this path than are others—some have realized a higher measure of Christhood. No one *is* a higher state of Christhood, but anyone may attain a higher realization of It than another at any given moment. There is no limitation to the measure of Christhood a person may express except the limitation which he himself places upon his own demonstration, and such limitation comes from believing that a person, in and of himself, has a demonstration to make which *he* can make, and of course, this is not true. Every demonstration to be made is always the demonstration of the activity of the Christ. We still use the word "I" too much, believing that "I" can do something, whereas "I" is but the instrument through which infinite Intelligence and divine Love function.

By bearing witness to God as the reality of being and by bearing witness to the impersonal nature of that which is appearing as evil, we reach a place in consciousness of no judgment, regardless of what suggestion may be presented to our thought in the form of a problem. The suggestion may appear as disease; it may appear as a man in prison with a mind separate and apart from God, a mind that can sin; or it may appear as careless drivers on the highway. The suggestion may appear in any form, but whatever the form, it is never anything more than a suggestion or a belief operating in the experience of the believer. As long as a person entertains the belief that there is an activity apart from God, a soul apart from God, a life, mind, or law apart from God, then it is as the Master said, "According to your faith be it unto you"[1]—in accordance with what you accept, so is your life experience unto you.

Most of us do not yet have a sufficiently developed confidence in the Infinite Invisible as a principle of life which becomes operative in our own individual experience through an activity of consciousness. We agree that there is a God—that under one name or another, God is—but we have not yet arrived at a deep enough conviction that this God, this Infinite Invisible, is operating in and through us and is the very life of our being. Having once attained the conscious realization of God, we have attained Its presence unto eternity. Our difficulty lies in our

[1] Matthew 9:29.

failure to recognize that there can be no success for us until we have achieved that conscious realization.

If we can bring ourselves to the point of God-realization through working out one problem after another, we need never again fear that God will leave us tomorrow. We shall be dwelling in the secret place of the most High, secure in the realization of the Infinite Invisible, safe in our union with God. Once that realization is attained, there is the continuous assurance: "*I* will never leave me nor forsake me. As *I* was with Abraham, Isaac, Jacob, Jesus, John, and Paul, so *I* will be with me. Even in the desert experiences, *I* will be with me."

Do not make the mistake of believing that it is possible for God to desert you or to be absent from your experience. You may desert God by becoming so immersed in "this world" that you fail to abide in the Word, but God never deserts you. Had you been present when Jesus was nailed to the Cross, when John was exiled to the island of Patmos, or when Paul was imprisoned in Rome, you might have felt that God had certainly deserted them. If you had seen Peter in chains, you might have accepted it as a desertion on the part of God. If you had been standing beside the Christians who were thrown to the lions, you might have marvelled that they had the fortitude to endure such persecution.

Every martyr who has gone to imprisonment or death has been at a place in consciousness where he has seen through the illusion of death and realized that there is no death. So when the martyrs were thrown into the lions' den or thrust into the fiery furnace, they had no thought whatsoever of dying:

They had already come to the realization of the Christian message of the immortality of life. They had relinquished all desire and risen to the vision of immortality, of life eternal—to the realization that there is no death. In that vision, prison, oil, and crucifixion were not terrors; they were not ordeals: They were opportunities for proving the nothingness of death, destruction, and all the temptations of "this world".

And what of us? Suppose that we do have a problem of disease? Suppose that we are meeting with lack and limitation? Why be concerned and why struggle as if we must get rid of those problems when our function is to prove the nothingness of them? Therein lies the secret. If our function is to prove the nothingness of all the appearances that the world calls discords, then why should we be concerned when another opportunity comes to us to prove their nothingness, first to ourselves and, then, to our world? If we could go about our work today with an absolute conviction that neither sin, disease, nor death were reality, we would never be concerned when called upon to face such appearances. Our response would be, "How can I be concerned when my very life is being devoted to proving the nothingness of that which appears as sin, disease, death, lack, and limitation? Whatever the appearance that comes to me, to my family, patients, or students, even though they be appearances comparable to those of Jesus on the Cross, John on Patmos, Paul in prison, or Peter in chains, I will say, 'Thank you, Father. Thank you that I have been given the awareness of the nothingness of this so that I am not trying to get

rid of it or to overcome it. I am grateful to have the opportunity to bear witness that this is nothing.' "
When, in your own personal experience or in the experience of your friends, family, patients, or students you are able to show the world that all the appearances it has been dreading, including the final enemy, are not real but only appearances, do you not see that in that way, and only in that way, can the world be awakened to the realization of spiritual truth?

To This End Was I Born

This is the moment in which it must become apparent to us that our study has not been for the purpose of overcoming sin, disease, death, lack, and limitation, but that we have been studying, meditating, and pondering these great spiritual truths so that we can realize that sin, disease, death, lack, and limitation exist only as appearances and not as reality. We see them not as problems, but as further opportunities. None of the early martyrs thought it a problem to die for his teaching: To them, it was an opportunity to show the world that there is no death. We, too, must welcome every opportunity that presents itself to prove to the world that death is an illusion and disease is not a reality: They are not to be feared and they are not to be hated.

Is sin, is disease, is death a reality? Does any one of these have actual existence? Do they have laws to maintain and sustain them? From the spiritual standpoint, the answer is: "No! 'Thou couldest have no power at all against me, except it were given thee from above.' "[1] Those are beautiful words, encouraging

[1] John 19:11.

words, inspiring words! But an hour from now the stomach pains or the head aches or the foot, and then how often our response is, "Why did this happen to me? Why should I have this problem?" Can you not see that this is why we have been studying, this is the moment, the very moment for which we have been preparing? This is our opportunity—the opportunity to meet every appearance of discord with the realization of its true nature, the realization that it is nothingness parading as something.

When the suggestion comes, whether it comes through someone calling on the telephone or whether it comes as a call from our own child or our own body, let us approach it in this same way: "This is not a problem; this is not something to deplore: This is the very thing for which I have been living; this is the very end to which I have been devoting hours upon hours of study and money—the opportunity to show the world that those things that it has been fearing and hating have no power whatsoever, no presence except in the delusion caused by my ignorance and miseducation.

"Out of my years of study, have I arrived at the conviction that disease has no law, sin has no law, poverty has no law, lack has no law? Have I come to the conclusion that the allness of God makes every sense of discord just that, a *sense* of discord and not a discord? Have I achieved the realization that the allness of God precludes the possibility of a selfhood apart from God, a will apart from God, a law apart from God?"

If we can answer these questions in the affirmative,

we can sit in our home or in our office and let a thousand people come to us for help knowing that they are all coming for only one purpose: to gain from our conviction an assurance that this appearance is not what it appears to be, is not what it claims to be, is not law, cause, or being. Even if we, ourselves, are confronted with these temptations, whether in the form of sin, disease, or the final enemy itself, we shall be able to appraise the situation with complete detachment: "I have been studying, praying, and meditating, and all to one end—to bring myself to the realization that appearances are not destructive, that appearances are not power. Whether that appearance is Pilate, whether it is the lion with its terrible jaws, whether it is infection or contagion, or whether it is economic depression or economic boom, I have been in training for years to face just such situations with the acknowledgment, 'Thank you, Father; Thou art, and nothing else is.' " Seeing through these appearances, we maintain the same divine indifference the martyrs had in facing the lions, the boiling oil, the crucifix, the prison, or the scourge: "These are shadows of mortal thought; they are not realities; they are images of human belief. They are not person; they are not place; they are not thing; they are not condition."

There Is No Power in Problems

Only those who attain such spiritual vision as the Master had or as Paul, John, Peter, and Joseph achieved can face the discords of human life with a smile on their faces and say, "You meant it for evil;

God meant it for good." There is no such thing as reality to the discords of human experience, and so it is that when we no longer fear them or hate them, but begin to understand their nature, then we, too, will be willing to suffer the martyr's fate, but only for one purpose—to prove that there is no death, to prove to the world that neither disease nor death has the power to end individual consciousness, life, and being.

Let us approach this matter of problems from that higher light. Let us first of all understand that we have been devoting years—many, many years—to the study of spiritual things, and for what purpose? To bring ourselves ultimately to the realization that those things that the world fears and hates are not even power. That is the object of our study; that is the purpose to which we are devoting ourselves. We are not seeking a new religion: We are seeking a principle of life, a principle by which to live.

Do you believe that you will ever find happiness, success, or joy until you have awakened to the realization that God is the only power? Even if you find a new and better way of healing disease, reforming sinners, or achieving prosperity, do you think for a moment that it will help you permanently? No, ways come and ways go, but as long as there is a belief in two powers, you will never know what it is to find your eternal peace. As long as you entertain a single trace of the belief that something can destroy your life or your child's life or your patient's life or your student's life, today or twenty years from now, you can never know rest or true peace. It is only when you come to the ultimate revelation and final realization that God is the only power and besides Him there is no power that your shoulders relax. Only then do you settle back in a state of peaceful relaxation, cushioned on that spiritual cloud of realization: "Now, I am home in Thee. Now, I know that there is nothing to fear. There is nothing for which to use God-power; there are no conditions or persons against which to use God-power." That is the ultimate secret.

You will not, however, arrive at that state of consciousness until enough problems have presented themselves to you, either your own problems or those of others, until all manner of temptation has been hurled at you—all manner of disease, all manner of sin, all manner of poverty, all manner of wealth—and not one of these temptations disturbs you. You do not look upon them as problems. How can they be problems if there is no power in them? Can you see, then, that you will not fear what may happen to anybody? You will not even fear what may happen to yourself. You will now realize a principle of life:

> * Thank You, Father. All that God is, I am; all that the Father hath is mine. Where I am, God is; where God is, I am. I and the Father are one. The whole kingdom of God is within me.

Then, with or without purse or scrip, you can move to any place in the world, go wheresoever God leads you, and always find yourself in the very presence of God. And in that Presence you will find the miracle: The presence of God will be interpreted tangibly to you as somebody bringing you food in the wilderness, or as rescue, safety, security, companionship, or peace.

However, until you come to the realization that there is no separation—there is no danger, there is no division—until you come to that realization, you will have problems. They will not really be problems, since there can be no separation from God. Since "I and my Father are one,"[1] what difference does it make in any person's life what the appearance is, because it is inevitable that God must appear as person, place, thing, circumstance, and condition, and always at the very moment It is needed? What difference could it make to an individual what the outer appearances are if he has the conviction that God constitutes his being?

Problems are problems only to the person who does not know the principle of life. The person who is not aware that there is a principle of life or who does not know what that principle of life is always has a problem, but to the person who has attained the realization of the Christ-message, there are no problems. That person can face the lion's jaws; he can face the Red Sea; he can face the wilderness-experience; he can face the valley of the shadow of death without calling it a problem. Why? Because "Thou art there." That is the answer which lifts every problem out of the category of a problem:

> * Thou art there. I have been studying and practicing all these years to be able to laugh at this that comes to me as a problem so that I can now say with conviction, "I know you; you are not

[1] John 10:30.

what you appear to be. I neither hate you, nor fear you, nor love you. I do not even respect you enough to deny you." I have now come to an awareness that God is the only power, so the whole world can bring its problems to me because to me they are not problems. I know there is no power in disease; there is no activity which can express as disease; there is no law of disease; and there is no reality in death. Whereas before I was blind, now I see.

This is not a problem. This is an opportunity to show the world that there are no problems, and that what appears as sin, disease, or death is but a sense of separation from God. I do not have to fight these problems; I do not have to overcome them; I do not have to rise above them or destroy them: "I have overcome the world."[1] Now the world can never again present any condition, person, or circumstance that I shall ever be tempted to fight, to destroy, or to overcome. Now I can look at the appearance and see through it.

Problems Represent a Sense of Separation from God

There are no problems once we have made our contact with God. Problems are a part of our experience only in so far as we have not made and maintained a conscious contact or union with God, a conscious oneness with God. We were all born with a sense of separation from God, and it is for this reason that anything can happen to us any time between the cradle and the grave—anything of an unpleasant nature as well as of a pleasant nature. In

[1] John 16:33.

the sense of separation from God, there is not the God-care, the God-sustenance, and the God-maintenance which are our rightful heritage as children of God.

We may at times have the experience of making contact with God, feeling the bliss of union with God; and we may even have long periods of living in the very presence of God and yet from time to time have problems; but these problems will represent the sense of separation from God that has crept in through universal mesmerism, that is, through universal world-beliefs. Understanding this, it becomes our lifework as seekers or searchers after God to retire as often as we can into that secret place of the most High, that inner sanctuary of our own being, and there re-establish our conscious union with God so that God's presence may so overshadow us that no other presence remains.

All the experiences of human existence come to us because of a belief in two powers, a power called good and a power called evil. We have learned, however, that there is no actual power in evil except such power as universal belief gives it, and we experience evil only because of our acceptance of universal belief. Problems disappear out of our experience, then, in proportion as we attain that mind which was also in Christ Jesus—the realization of God as the only power and the only law. This really means that the laws which we have feared—laws of climate, weather, food, germs, infection, contagion, accident—are not laws at all but rather a sense of law with no power except such power as universal belief gives them.

God does not send us problems. Under no circumstances, under no conditions, and at no time, does God ever give us a problem. In this understanding, we welcome the circumstances and people which appear to us as problems because of the opportunity they furnish us to rise into that spiritual realization and spiritual kingdom in which we find no problems, no evil law, no destructive power, and no harmful presence.

Very often people experience long years of good physical health and a satisfactory sense of supply, believing that they are living in God's grace, when actually they are merely enjoying the accidental health and wealth of human experience. It is for this reason that even though, at any given time, we may be enjoying good health or abundant supply, we must retire within ourselves at regular intervals of the day to assure ourselves that we are depending on the activity of God for our health—on the presence, the power, and the light of God. We must retire into that inner sanctuary within our own being and there realize that we are not dependent on husband, wife, position, or investments for our supply, but that our supply is the grace of God and is with us regardless of any outer appearance, circumstance, condition, or person.

Should we for any reason experience a period of illness or of lack or limitation, let us be very quick to realize that this has come to us as a part of our experience only so that we can rise above these adverse circumstances as quickly as possible in the realization of our conscious oneness with God. Let us not fight these errors of sense, but rather rest in the realization that these have come only because we have been entertaining a sense of separation from God; we have been entertaining a sense of a selfhood apart from God; we have been entertaining a sense of a law apart from spiritual law.

There Are No Problems

Problems are not problems any more when there is no longer a desire to attain anything in this world. When there are no desires, there are no problems. What then becomes of the desire for health, supply, and companionship? Are we not to desire these? The answer to that depends upon how far along we have come in spiritual unfoldment. Tens of thousands of copies of Infinite Way writings have been purchased by seekers, but only a very few thousand copies of *The Infinite Way Letters of 1954, 1955, 1956,* and *1957*, and the reason is that these few thousands are probably the only people among all our readers who have reached the stage where, if there is a single desire remaining, it is only the desire to know God "whom to know aright is life eternal." These volumes of *Letters* and The Infinite Way Wisdoms which are found in the latest edition of *The Infinite Way* are undoubtedly the deepest of all The Infinite Way writings, and it is for this reason that they can never be widely popular. They contain the specific principles which, when studied, assimilated, and practiced, actually produce the state of desirelessness.

Do not think for a moment that a state of desirelessness takes from you the joy of life, for I can tell you from my own experience that every day of the week is a thrilling experience to me, from the joyous expectancy I feel when I first awaken in the morning to the final moment of peace which comes as I fall asleep. To live without desire is to live a vital life of alert expectancy. It is like going out into the garden or into the park in the springtime to observe the buds which have become flowers; or it is like being up before sunrise, waiting for that first glimpse of dawn, and then watching the sun rise on the horizon. In all of this, there is no desire or anxiety because there is a calm conviction that these things will come to pass. In the conviction that God's grace is our sufficiency, how can we have any desires? In the assurance that the Lord is my shepherd, that He leadeth me beside the still waters and maketh me to lie down in green pastures, what room is left for desire?

This is the third stage of unfoldment, a stage in which, in reality, there are no problems. Even though situations may arise in our experience which must be met, we do not look upon them as problems. They are not problems because we know the answer, and in knowing the answer, we are able to watch what was heretofore called a problem resolve itself into the harmony that actually exists. When we arrive at that stage, we are at an advanced state of spiritual unfoldment. That time never comes as long as there is a desire for any earthly thing. It makes no difference what the desire is or how good it may be. People often ask, "Do you mean that it isn't right to desire good health, or it isn't right to desire abundant supply or a beautiful home?" From the human standpoint, it is very right; but from a spiritual standpoint, it can never be right because desire is the acknowledgment of a lack. No student is very far advanced in spiritual unfoldment if he is aware of a lack.

Eventually every aspirant on the spiritual path must come to a place where he realizes, " 'My kingdom is not of this world'[1]—God's kingdom is not of this world," and with that revelation comes the further realization, "What is there of this world that I desire or need? What is there of this world that I want? What is there that I lack? In my desire for something of this world, am I not perpetuating the belief that something of this world can satisfy me or complete my experience or do something for me?" Can you not see that our problems are born through our desire for place, position, wealth—for something beyond our present reach?

Ponder this subject of problems; meditate upon it until every phase of this subject has clarified itself within your consciousness. Then in the measure that this spiritual awareness becomes an integral part of your being, will the harmonies and the discords of human existence disappear from your experience, and you will find yourself in the atmosphere of God where spiritual harmonies and only spiritual harmonies are present. You are then living a spiritual life, derived from the one spiritual Source, maintained and sustained by spiritual law, and shared with those on the spiritual path. The world will see its fruits but will never comprehend the glory of the inner joy and peace which come with the realization that our good is not dependent upon any person; our good is experienced in our conscious oneness with

[1] John 18:36.

God, completely separate and apart from any person, circumstance, situation, or condition. Our good is the unfolding of God as our consciousness.

It is inevitable that we should be lifted higher in spiritual living if we see that every problem we solve is a foundation for the unfolding of a greater depth of spiritual vision. If we will look upon our day to day experiences in this way, each today will be a continuous unfoldment of God's glory. The depth of our vision will continue to bring forth greater and greater spiritual light, wisdom, and guidance; so that every day will be a day of deeper discernment, a day more completely dedicated to living in the atmosphere of God than was the day before.

ACROSS THE DESK

Christmas at Halekou has been a truly joyous season with meditation and healing work the keynote. Several students have been here from the mainland, plus a few local students, and this has added up to a great many meditation periods every day, with healing and an increasing depth of meditation as the theme of the work. There is every reason to expect finer healing work than ever before, because more of us are uniting in this work. There are far less calls for help from our class-taught students and their families, and more of these students are prepared to help others. Before I leave the Christmas scene, may I add a sincere "thank you" to all of you for your holiday greetings and your messages of appreciation for The Infinite Way.

In the New Year, I ask every student to study *daily* the chapter, "Love Thy Neighbor," in *Practicing the Presence.*[1] This will open a limitless vision, if you will continue to ponder, contemplate, and assimilate the essence of this chapter. It is deeper than you think. Furthermore, be sure to include daily work with "Protection," as outlined in *The 1955 Infinite Way Letters.*[2]

By now, the nature of problems should be better understood. Wherever you are in consciousness—whether problems are still problems to you or whether they are opportunities—remember that you must work your way, through demonstration, up to the final step of spiritual realization. Our students must not believe that merely "stating," "affirming," or "thinking" that problems are unreal is the demonstration. First, learn the correct letter of truth, then practice it every minute of the day and night, and finally attain the actual realization which is demonstration. The way is straight and narrow if you wish to be of the few who finally enter the kingdom, or realization, of God.

[1] By the author. *Practicing the Presence* (New York: Harper & Brothers, 1958), pp. 66-81.
[2] By the author. *The Infinite Way Letters 1955* (London, England: L. N. Fowler & Co., Ltd. 1956) pp. 39-45.

Author's note: Wherever the word "I" is italicized, the reference is to God.

CHAPTER THREE: MARCH

THE PRACTICE OF SPIRITUAL HEALING

To be successful in spiritual healing, it is necessary to come out and be separate—to adopt a clear principle from which there is no deviation. In order to be free and to free others, you yourself must know the nature of spiritual healing. The correct premise for healing is that God constitutes individual being, individual you and me; God constitutes your being and mine; and there is nothing which can defile that pure spiritual being. There is no cause save one: "Hear, O Israel: The Lord our God is one Lord."[1]

Spiritual healing cannot be based on the fact that there is something to be removed and that, in order to remove it, you must find its cause and then get rid of its effect. Nowhere in the New Testament does the Master indicate that there is a mental cause for physical disease; nowhere does he say to anyone, "You are ill because of this, that, or the other thing"; nowhere does he say that you are being held in bondage to this error because of that error; nowhere does he say that there is a cause for disease. Rather he demonstrated irrefutably his firm conviction that disease is not a power: "Stretch forth thine hand.[2] . . . Woman, thou art loosed from thine infirmity.[3] . . . Lazarus, come forth."[4] Do these

[1] Deuteronomy 6:4.
[2] Matthew 12:13.
[3] Luke 13:12.
[4] John 11:43.

words indicate that sickness has a cause or that disease was created by God?

Spiritual healing is an acknowledgment of God as the infinity of being, as the infinity of your being and mine. Anything unlike God which presents itself to us is merely a state of mesmerism, a suggestion coming to us for our acceptance or rejection. It makes no difference whether the suggestion comes in the form of a sin or a disease, of unemployment or lack, the treatment is the same—the recognition that we are not dealing with physical conditions, but that we are dealing purely with a state of hypnotism. When we realize that, a large percentage of our healing work is accomplished. Then, can it make any difference whether it is a right leg or a left one, a stomach or a back, a head or a foot?

Spiritual healing has nothing to do with bodies; it has nothing to do with unemployed people, poor people, homeless people, or friendless people. Spiritual healing has to do with prayer, with the recognition and acknowledgment of our infinite and perfect nature. Prayer is our ability to attain conscious oneness with God, to be receptive and responsive to that which is called the still small voice, or spiritual impulse within us—the Christ.

Discord Is a State of Mesmerism

As long as our thought is hypnotized into looking at a body or a pocketbook, we shall not break the mesmerism that will give us our freedom. As long as we are trying to treat the body or find a cause for sin, disease, or lack, we shall be in the very dream that we have been in and are trying to break. It would be like dreaming that we are drowning in the water and then calling out for someone to drain the ocean dry so that we could walk ashore. In such a case, it is only necessary for someone to awaken us from the dream. Upon awakening, we learn that we are not in the water and never were in the water. In spiritual healing, it is much the same; it is only necessary for someone to waken us from the mesmeric dream of human existence for us to achieve our freedom.

Spiritual healing is a realization of God. It is an inner communion with the Divine in which, or through which, the assurance comes to us that God is on the scene. Then these illusory pictures begin to disappear. If, when someone asks for help, we should say, "You are suffering because you are so unloving or because you are so unreasonable or because you haven't enough gratitude," that person will continue to be imprisoned in the very dream that he would like to have dissolved. The Master overcame the world by learning the nature of that with which he was dealing. He did not try to find a cause for the death of Lazarus. He did not try to find a cause of the illness of Peter's mother-in-law, nor did he attribute it to old age: He awakened her out of the dream and brought her back. When the corpse of the young man was being carried past him, he did not stop to ask what had caused the death or what had caused the disease: He just brought that young man up off his bier.

In Infinite Way practice, we are not dealing with sick or sinful people or with poor people, nor are we trying to improve them. Our task is realizing the nature of all these discords and waking out of them. The best way to do this is to understand, once and for all, that we are not dealing with a condition or a person: We are dealing with a state of mesmerism. Then, if we drop the problem right there, we shall find that sixty percent of the ills will disappear with no further treatment. Another twenty percent will disappear when we go within and ponder the nature of God, gaining a clear realization of what God actually is and of the whole nature of error as but a dream—universal hypnotism—not a condition or a person. Some measure of a material sense of existence will still cling to those who persist in a material way of living. We need not concern ourselves with those few, however, because their number is small.

When help is needed for yourself or for others, immediately remember that this call has nothing to do with a person or with a condition. This is the Adam-dream, or fall of man. This is the mesmerism of the world and nothing else. Stop with that; turn from the picture; hold fast to that realization; and do not allow your thought to go back to the person or the condition. Then, if there is not an instantaneous healing and if help is needed or asked for again, remind yourself once more that this is not a person, this is not a condition: This is an attempt to hypnotize you into seeing error in a world of God's creating, and you must refuse to acknowledge any error in God's universe.

It is not necessary to know the name of the person who is asking for help, nor the name or nature of the disease or whether it is an appearance of disease, sin, fear, lack or limitation, or unemployment. It is only necessary to know that there is a call for help. When the call comes, the first thing to remember is that this has nothing to do with the person asking for help; this has nothing to do with a condition: This is a temptation coming to you to accept a world apart from God, to accept a creation apart from God or a life or a law apart from God, and you must refuse to be confused by that.

Go into meditation, then, and after pondering the nature of God and the nature of the Christ, the nature of error and the nothingness of all appearances, wait. Wait for that one second of deep breath or inner peace. That should bring the healing.

Understand the Nature of Specific Work

The effectiveness of this procedure is based on the assumption that, because of your study and consistent practice, you do know the nature of specific work for specific problems. For example, in your study of the principles of The Infinite Way, you have learned that God constitutes individual being, that God is the only law operating in individual consciousness, that Spirit is the only cause, and that consciousness is the only creative principle. You know from this that disease is a claim of mental or material law and, therefore, you recognize its nothingness. You know that disease is a claim of a creation and of a selfhood apart from the divine Consciousness. You know that disease is a claim of a life separate and apart from the one God-life and, in your preparatory years of study, you have become so assured of this that you need not handle it specifically with every call that comes to you, although when necessary you do handle it in just that way. Similarly, any claim of lack or limitation stems from the universal belief that supply consists of getting, but by now you have learned that you demonstrate supply only in proportion to your giving. You need not necessarily handle this with every claim of lack, limitation, or unemployment that comes to you, but you should be prepared to do this and you should be prepared to explain it to your patient if this seems wise.

The calls for help that come to you regarding human relationships whether in business, family, or community life are usually in the nature of misunderstandings or lonesomeness or lack of friends. Here again the claim is one of believing that good must come to a person, instead of understanding that all good flows out from the individual to the world. The healing consists of the realization that since God constitutes individual being, all good flows out *from* the individual, not *to* him. It is not necessary to know this specific truth each time this claim comes to you, but it is necessary that, as a practitioner, you have this awareness and when necessary, realize this specific truth in treatment and, furthermore, explain it to the patient when it seems wise.

Actually, then, during your years of preparatory study, you must learn the principles which constitute the message of The Infinite Way. You must know the specific truth regarding every claim so that this truth forms your consciousness anew. Then you will often find that, when called upon for help, you will not have to know certain truths specifically every time, although there will be many times when it will be necessary to be very specific.

A more comprehensive presentation of the subject of spiritual healing is found in the British edition of *The Master Speaks* which states, "This very book . . . based on the teachings of the Master, Christ Jesus, is ideally suited to the purpose of serving as a textbook for the teaching of spiritual living and spiritual healing—and may be used by any church denomination, any university healing activity, or by any other group interested in this subject."[1] The chapters, "Reality of Spirit,"[2] "A High Form of Treatment,"[3] and "Healing and Silence"[4] will prove valuable to the serious student who is striving to gain a clearer understanding of the principles and practice of spiritual healing.

Practical Instructions to Workers

There are occasions when it is necessary to repeat treatments many, many times. Some cases are so obstinate that you will have to treat for a year before you break down whatever it is that is unyielding in the case. Whether you meet it instantaneously, whether you have to work two days, or whether you have to work on one case a whole year, this is the way it is done.

Never be tempted to blame yourself or your patient for any lack of healing. Never use the words, "you," "he," or "she." At least be as fair to your

[1] By the author. *The Master Speaks* (London, England: George Allen & Unwin, 1957), p. 11.

[2] *Ibid.*, pp. 29-45.

[3] *Ibid.*, pp. 144-160.

[4] *Ibid.*, pp. 257-270.

human patient as you would be to your cat or dog or bird if it were sick. If your pet—your dog, cat, or bird—were sick, how would you go about treating it? Would you ask your dog whether he had been sinning or ungrateful or unloving or unjust? Would you tell him to read twelve pages in your favorite book, or would you tell him that he must tithe or go to church? No, you would do no such thing. You would sit down in prayer and you would achieve your inner communion with God; and then your dog or your cat or your bird would jump up whole and perfect. There is nothing in animals which resists, and that is why they respond so quickly. Furthermore, you have a conviction that there is nothing in God's plan that would make an animal sick, and so you sit down and commune with God in order to feel God's presence, and the moment you have the consciousness of that Presence, your dog or your cat is well.

Be that fair to your patient, to your student, or to the members of your family. Do not put the responsibility on their shoulders. That does not mean that you can go up and down this world healing everybody whom you would like to see well. Everyone has the right to choose his own method of cure, and there are some who have not a sufficient degree of receptivity to respond to spiritual healing.

When someone asks you for help, sit down and have your God-realization even if, at the moment, he seems humanly unworthy. It is not for you to judge and it is not for me to judge. There is only one thing that matters: Somebody has asked for help, and you are obligated to do your best to give it to him. That does not mean filling your day with unnecessary interviews because healing has nothing to do with interviews. Healing can best be done when there are no interviews, when those doing the healing work are left alone to be free in their meditations and prayers. Healing work does not require the physical proximity of patient and practitioner. As a matter of fact, healing work is usually far more easily accomplished without it, although there are a few exceptions to that rule, and each one who is working must find that out for himself. Sometimes, I have found that, when there is no response to absent work, an occasional present treatment is helpful. Interviews are only necessary either at the time of the first visit to help the patient find his way or later for the purpose of helping him in instruction.

When it comes to instruction, never forget that it is your function to reveal to your patients or students the necessity of "dying daily" to their human qualities and of being reborn into spiritual consciousness. I might illustrate that this way: When a person so lives an impersonal cause, whether it be some form of service to mankind or devotion to a church or some spiritual teaching, he could never impoverish himself, regardless of how much of his income he gave to it. In fact, many have discovered that they have actually enriched themselves by this giving. Since this sounds like the very opposite of everything that is called common sense, you can understand how difficult a task it is even to bring yourself to this realization and demonstration; but, until you do, it is not likely that you will help others with their problems of lack or limitation. After you have proved this principle for yourself, teach it to your patients and students. *Remember, it is only your own demonstrated state of spiritual consciousness which can help another, and not just the words you learn from a book.*

When people want instruction on how to study, how to meditate, or how to live the spiritual life, then is the time to begin interviews. Those interviews at first should be short because no individual can carry away with him more than one or two spiritual ideas. They should have an opportunity to put such teaching as has been given them into practice, and then come back at a later day for something further.

Watch that you do not sit in judgment on those who turn to you for help. Do not criticize; do not condemn; do not tell them that they did this, that, or the other thing. The Infinite Way ministry is a prayer ministry, not a method of psychological healing. It has nothing to do with finding the error in the patient's thought; it has nothing to do with who or what brought this condition about. The Infinite Way has to do with prayer which, in its final stage, is an actual, concrete feeling or realization of God's presence. When we reach that stage, then regardless of the name or nature of the claim, it must begin to evaporate.

The Subject of Matter

Students of metaphysics often find difficulty in solving their problems of health because of a misunderstanding concerning the nature of their bodies which in its turn is based on a misunderstanding of the nature of matter.

In the early days of modern metaphysics, it was the practice to deny matter. Much was written about the unreality of matter, and this led to a denial of the body, to the doctrine of the unreality of the body, and in many cases to the desire to overcome the body or get rid of the body. It must be understood that while our unenlightened concepts of God, life, man, and body form the illusions of sense, nevertheless, God made all that was made and all that God made is good, and therefore, from this standpoint, everything that exists must partake of the nature of God.

Physical science has revealed that matter itself is indestructible and that matter never had a beginning and that matter can never have an end. Matter changes forms but, according to the scientists of today, matter never began nor can it ever end; and of course this reveals not only the indestructibility of matter, but actually the immortality of matter. Unless the nature of matter, its origin and that which is its substance and governing power, can be discovered, we are left in as much of a dilemma as when we denied matter but did not understand what we were doing or why.

The Infinite Way reveals that mind is matter. Mind is the substance of that which the world calls matter, and it is for this reason that mind governs and controls matter. Mind imbued with truth produces harmonious matter—form or body. Mind imbued with error—with ignorance, with falsities about God, life, man, body, and matter—produces inharmonious, discordant matter or body.

While this may appear to you as a revolutionary

idea, since it has not been revealed to you in this way before, nevertheless, we have been witnessing the proof of this in the past seventy-five years of metaphysical healing in situations where an individual, acting as a practitioner and knowing the truth, has produced harmony in a body where discord and inharmony had existed until the request for help. Every form of disease has at some time or another, been met by metaphysical treatment, that is, by knowing the truth. Knowing the truth has transformed inactive bodies into active ones, diseased organs into healthy organs, diseased brains into harmonious-acting brains; it has reduced fevers, removed tumors, eliminated infection, and, in every possible manner, has transformed sick bodies into well bodies by the process of knowing the truth.

Sometimes this has been construed to mean that mind governs matter or that mind governs the body, but this is only partly true because the full truth is that mind is matter and mind constitutes the substance of which the body is formed. It is for this reason that mind, imbued with truth, reveals the harmony of mind and body, whereas mind, imbued with untruth, false theories and ignorance, produces the discords of human experience.

Governing the body through the activity of truth consciously known through the mind, however, is but a beginning step toward spiritual development, unfoldment, and demonstration. Above the realm of the conscious, thinking mind, is the universal Spirit where Consciousness Itself, without the benefit of words or thoughts, governs individual life, including the body, harmoniously, joyously, prosperously.

It is difficult to attain this higher state of consciousness in which life is spiritually lived until one has been through the preliminary step of understanding that mind is the substance of the physical body and that mind imbued with truth will result in a completely transformed body.

Relation of Spiritual Living to Spiritual Healing

Spiritual healing and spiritual living are inseparable; they go hand in hand. The source of healing is the consciousness of the individual who is at the moment acting as practitioner. Let it be understood that, if the effect is to be pure, the source must be kept free and pure. Naturally, the best results will flow forth from the purest consciousness, and therefore a person expecting to bring about healing must live up to certain standards before this can be accomplished. Students should give serious study to the chapter on "The Healing Ministry" in *The Master Speaks.*[1]

For this reason, every student on the spiritual path must have a period of preparation before entering upon healing work. This preparation consists of two parts: first, the study of the correct letter of truth; and second, the self-discipline which such a path involves. During this period of preparation, it is necessary to study the Sermon on the Mount and to attempt, as fast as possible, to release yourself from such conduct as is described in those passages which begin, "Ye have heard that it was

[1] By the author. *The Master Speaks,* 127-143.

said by them of old . . ."[1] and then watch and see to what degree your life begins to conform to those parts which begin with, "But I say unto you . . ."[2]

As your consciousness is purged of hate, animosity, resentment, jealousy, envy, self-seeking, self-glorification, etcetera, it becomes a fit instrument for spiritual healing. It is during this period of preparation that you must adjust yourself to the idea of God as one power and, at the same time, give up the conventional belief that God is a great power which can be used to destroy evil powers.

You will be able to heal successfully only in proportion to your willingness to "die daily" to all the traits of character which constitute humanhood and to be reborn into spiritual consciousness, a consciousness which contains neither love, hate, nor fear of evil. Let no one believe that he can be the same human being that he has heretofore been and yet be successful in spiritual healing. The reason we have so few spiritual healers is that there are so few people who are ready to undertake this preparatory period of study and practice; there are so few who are willing to undergo the self-discipline which removes their lives from the law of the Ten Commandments and lifts them into the atmosphere of grace—into the atmosphere of but two commandments: "Thou shalt love the Lord thy God with all thy heart, and with all thy soul, and with all thy mind. . . . Thou shalt love thy neighbor as thyself."[3]

It is only in the surrender of the human sense of life that the full spiritual heritage can become

[1] Matthew 5:21. [2] Matthew 5:22. [3] Matthew 22:37, 39.

manifest in our experience. Spiritual healing, without some measure of spiritual living, is almost unthinkable and almost impossible. The spiritual way of life is a reversal of the human way of life. Human beings nearly always want something; they are nearly always trying to get something. Human living is based largely on getting: getting supply, getting health, getting companionship, getting married or getting unmarried, getting a home, getting away for a vacation or getting back—getting, getting, getting, always getting. The essence of human experience could almost be summed up in some such way as this: What can I add to myself? In what way can I increase my good? In what way can I acquire more?

Living the Spiritual Life

Spiritual living is the reverse of all that. Spiritual living begins with the premise that I and the Father are one and that all that the Father has is mine. Spiritual living, therefore, begins with the realization that we are already infinite, that we already embrace within ourselves all of the good that God has to bestow. Such a realization immediately removes all desire to get, to accomplish, or to achieve.

How can a person come into this living experience of his divine inheritance? Truly, the answer is very simple. There is a way—the Master has pointed the way very clearly—but it is the putting into practice of that way which is the stumbling block. Why? Look about you. Look into your own heart. See with what tenacity human beings clutch to themselves their possessions. This is what makes the practice of the Christ-teaching so difficult. But now, turn ye—"Turn ye, and live."

Begin to loose that which you already have in such infinite abundance; cast your bread upon the waters. Instead of seeking love, love; be loving; find some way, some place, somehow to express love. Instead of seeking cooperation, begin to give cooperation. Instead of seeking blessings, seek to bless. Instead of seeking to get, seek to give. It makes no difference whether you begin with pennies, nickels, or dimes; it makes no difference if you begin by giving only fifteen minutes of service to someone in need of your service. What counts is that you make the acknowledgment:

> *All that the Father has is mine. Right now, the place whereon I stand is holy ground. Nothing need be added to me. I am this instant in one of those many mansions of the Father's, even if appearances do not testify to this. "I and my Father are one."[1] In my true being, in my true identity, "I and my Father are one."
>
> God's nature is available to all who seek it. God's will is done on earth as it is in heaven, and there is no other will. God's will is the only will. God's will is the only will being done on earth as it is in heaven.
>
> Here and now, God's presence fulfills me; God's presence is the fulfillment of my whole life. To experience the realization of the presence of God, is to have my whole life fulfilled. God's grace is my sufficiency in all things, omnipresent where I am.

[1] John 10:30.

It is not absent from me; it does not have to be attained; God's grace need only be realized, and then it is my sufficiency in all things.

Our aim is to get nothing, to acquire nothing, to receive nothing except a continuous realization of God's presence. That must be done three, four, or five times a day—as many times as we can find two or three minutes to steal away alone just for the realization of God's presence. In the human picture, we look to the world for what we need. Some people find themselves dependent upon their jobs or their employers; some are dependent on business; some are dependent on husbands or wives; some are dependent on climate and weather; some are dependent on the government. The spiritual picture is the reverse of that: "Thy grace, God's grace, is my sufficiency." That breaks every human tie and every human bond. We continue to associate with each other and to share with each other, but we no longer have a dependence on each other. Spiritual living means that every service of wife, husband, mother, or father is performed through love, not through duty or necessity. There is now only one necessity—to receive God's grace.

If you are living spiritually, you are losing your dependence on man whose breath is in his nostrils: You lose your dependence on weather and climate; you lose your dependence on money; and you acquire your complete freedom in the realization that I and the Father are one, that all that the Father has is mine, and that is why the place whereon I stand is holy ground. Remember this will not be true after a treatment. Treatment is merely to bring to light that which already is. Before Abraham was, this truth is and has been true of you. Wake up out of the Adam-dream—the belief that there is either good or evil in any form—and come into the realization of your spiritual sonship.

If we are children of God, we are heirs; and if heirs, joint-heirs with Christ in God. What can we need and whom can we need? Nothing but this realization. The realization of God's presence is what breaks the mesmeric sense of a selfhood apart from God, of a person apart from God, or a condition apart from God. This is the very realization that breaks the whole Adam-dream. When we wake up, we find that we are children of God and that we are really in heaven because when once we are freed of material dependencies, earth is heaven.

There is no other heaven than this; there is no other body than this. This is the perfect body which God gave you and the only reason that you find it disturbing is because you have allowed the mesmerism of this world to inflict itself upon you with its beliefs. Once you break that dream, you will be satisfied with this body. It will move about and do everything you tell it to do.

When you remove power from the form, you will find that it is literally true that God gave you dominion over this body, over everything on earth, everything in the air, everything beneath the waters. You will discover that that is true, and then you will be satisfied. The body will be a fine instrument to use, and you will be satisfied with it; the body will be so responsive to what you want it to do, when you want it to do it, that you will be grateful that you have this body.

This life you are living is the very life you have been seeking. You have been going places and doing things to find it, when all the time satisfaction and fulfillment were right here with you. It is you, yourself, who have permitted the mesmerism of good and evil to block it off from your view. Wake up. "Awake thou that sleepest . . . and Christ shall give thee light."[1] Awake and realize:

> *This is the very minute that God gave me. This is the body God gave me. This is the consciousness, the life, the Soul, the Spirit that God gave me. This is the infinity of supply that God gave me—all here, and all right where I am now.

As you abide in that truth and let that truth abide in you, the dream vanishes, and you really wake up to find that this is heaven. Sometimes in waking up, it moves you out of the physical or material environment to which you have been bound by the mesmerism of human existence. You then find yourself in green pastures and beside still waters, whereas before that you may have found yourself on a battlefield of some sort or other.

As you study The Infinite Way writings, try to understand what the message is: It is not the healing of minds, bodies, or pocketbooks; it is not physical healing or mental healing; it is awakening out of a dream and finding that now are we the sons of God. That is the essence of this message.

[1] Ephesians 5:14.

In mid-January we left Hawaii for Australia, stopping for re-fueling at Canton Island, an eight-mile long coral reef, 160 miles from the Equator, and then again at Nandi in the Fiji Islands. It was a beautiful, but somewhat bumpy flight. We were met at the airport at Sydney and soon found ourselves driving on a broad highway along the beach to inspect this very colorful chain of harbors and bays. It was such a hot summer day—94°—that we returned to the hotel at three o'clock in the afternoon. Less than two hours later an unannounced hurricane with a ninety-three mile an hour wind struck the city and the beaches which we had just visited. The storm was of short duration, lasting only fifteen minutes before moving out to the open sea. This was one of those unexpected experiences which give zest to travel and provide us with additional opportunities for practicing the principles of The Infinite Way.

Lectures and class work began Monday evening with a talk to a group of some sixty-five students in Sydney. You will be happy to know that all of the work in Australia and New Zealand is being recorded so that you, as well as the students in Australia, may have an opportunity to hear this message. The first talk was focused on the senselessness of the fears which are constantly being thrust upon us: fear of Russia; fear of bombs; fear of disease; and other forms of fear hysteria. Mass hysteria created a fear of the Kaiser and his submarines and a fear of Hitler and his "blitz." Stalin was a name which caused tremors throughout the earth; and now more fear—new dictators throughout the world and "outer space."

Is God a myth? Are we or are we not anchored in God? Is there power in the "arm of flesh"?[1] Is the creature—the form or effect—greater than the Creator, the invisible Spirit? Am *I* not more than all these? Do we no longer believe that "*I* will never leave thee, nor forsake thee"[2]—even when faced with bombs and tyrants? Must mankind succumb once again to a hopeless fear of "man, whose breath is in his nostrils: for wherein is he to be accounted of?"[3]

Students, be a light unto "a perverse nation" and stand fast in your faith that all power rests in the Invisible; let your confidence be rooted in the firm conviction that that which can be seen, heard, tasted, touched, or smelled is but the arm of flesh—nothingness. The fears of this world are not insuperable. The solution of the Russian situation should be the clearest demonstration of such a principle ever presented to a fear-ridden world because the lines are so sharply drawn: On one side, there is the atheistic claim that material force is power and on the other side the Christ-revelation that "the Father that dwelleth in me, he doeth the works."[4] Which of these is truth? Why not "stand still, and see the salvation of the Lord"?[5] Will you, an Infinite Way student, fear this challenge or will you meet it with a courage born of wisdom?

The Voice has told me that the theme of our forthcoming work might be in the nature of the following admonition: Do not try to mold God's will to your

[1] II Chronicles 32:8. [2] Hebrews 13:5.
[3] Isaiah 2:22. [4] John 14:10. [5] Exodus 14:13.

desires, but rather with faith yield yourself—your hopes, your desires, and your will—to God; do not pray for God to do your bidding or to serve you or your interests, but pray that you may be shown how to serve God and God's interests on earth.

One thing more the Voice has told me about which I may soon write, but until that moment comes, study the story of Sapphira, Acts 5:1-10.

CHAPTER FOUR: APRIL

THE MESSAGE OF EASTER: "I HAVE OVERCOME THE WORLD"

THE prophecy by Hebrew sages and seers of the Messiah, of the one who would come to bring deliverance from slavery, ignorance, sin, disease, and all discordant conditions, was something which could not be comprehended by the materialistic consciousness of that day. Only the spiritual leaders of the Hebrew people, who had come out of slavery, illiteracy, and gross spiritual ignorance, had been able to hold fast to the vision of one God. Their hundreds upon hundreds of years of consecration to that faith in the Infinite Invisible and their abiding realization and revelation of one God were finally rewarded by the evidence among them of the Messiah, of that Presence which dissolved all sin, sickness, and lack.

This very Messiah, or Christ, was made evident in Jesus by the healing of the sick, the raising of the dead, the opening of the eyes of the blind, and the unstopping of the ears of the deaf. Suddenly, that which the intellectuals of the day had considered nothing more than a superstitious belief of some ignorant Hebrews—folklore—became a living reality walking the earth, evident to all who had any measure of spiritual vision.

The effects of the appearance on earth of the Messiah were so startling that even though the materialists could not comprehend the significance of what they saw, instinctively they began to fight and battle the Messiah and ultimately sought to crucify It. Yes, they crucified the Christ, but they crucified It unto resurrection and ascension, not unto death. Now, two thousand years later, the secret of what happened on earth at that time has been discovered—how what the unillumined had called superstitious folklore became a living reality, and how today that very same Presence can become practical in the experience of those who have the vision to behold it. But once more, as of old, wherever the evidence of Its activity and ensuing fruitage is presented to material sense, material sense fights, battles, and seeks to destroy It.

Opposition to the Christ Comes from Within Ourselves

Today, however, we have gone a step further than those who lived 2000 years ago were able to take. Those who first caught the vision of the Christ in the Holy Land believed that the opposition to the Christ stemmed from the Hebrews of the church and from the government of Rome, that is, that the opposition was from *outside of themselves*—from others who did not understand them. Today a higher revelation has been given to us. Today we recognize that any opposition to the Christ experienced by us is taking place within our own consciousness. It may appear that the opposition comes from friends, relatives, governments, or churches, but that is a faulty assumption: The truth is that any opposition to the full development and demonstration of our Christhood comes from the materialistic side of our own nature, within our own being.

There is a Christ, and that Christ is our own spiritual consciousness, that He within us that performeth that which is given us to do. But at the very time that we know this and declare it and attempt to live it, there are forces *within us* which would seek to crucify the development and the expression of that Christhood. These forces constitute the materialistic side of our nature. Each one of us has some measure of material sense, whether or not we are sitting at the feet of Paul, John, or Jesus, or whether we have actually attained the height that Paul had reached when he saw that in his true identity he himself was beyond all sin even though a sense of sin operated within him. Even while we know that this true identity which is our own being governs, feeds, and sustains us, yet there is at the same time a side of us which still finds some parts of the human scene very good, and because it appears to be good, we seek to increase that very material sense which the Christ through Its activity would destroy.

The activity of the Christ in our consciousness destroys the errors of sense—the discord, the diseases, and the false appetites; but if you study The Infinite Way writings carefully, you will notice something which may have escaped you: This same Christ which destroys the errors of your experience also destroys the harmonies, joys, profits, and health of material sense. It destroys *both* the good and the evil of material sense and brings to light that which it was the purpose of the Messiah of old to reveal—not more of "this kingdom," not a better "this world," but "My kingdom" which is not of this world.

Rising Above Personal Sense

The underlying theme behind the parables and allegories which form a part of religion and philosophy is that there is a world behind this world, there is a life behind this life, there is a man behind this man. Behind what you see as a visible Joel, or what I see as a visible John or Mary, behind that individual or within the consciousness of that individual is his real Selfhood, the divinity of his being—that *I* which is truth, that *I* which is the child of God, that *I* which is the Messiah predicted of old. The *I* walks through a den of lions unharmed because the den of lions does not see the *I*. *I* walks the earth untouched by material happenings because the material mind of man does not see that *I*.

There is a portion of our being which is still material and which is in conflict with that part of us which is divine. Through the overcoming within ourselves of personal sense, ultimately we are able to say with the Master, "I have overcome the world."[1] Jesus did not overcome Rome; he did not overcome the Sanhedrin of the Hebrew church: He overcame the world. What world? "This world," the world of material sense within himself. He overcame the world within himself for his sake and for the benefit of all those who were attuned to his state of consciousness and were able to behold the vision

[1] John 16:33.

which we call the Christ, or Christhood—the vision of our divine Self.

In proportion as we overcome the material side of our own being, as we overcome that part of us which still seeks to enrich ourselves, to ennoble ourselves, or in some way to glorify our human identity, in that degree have we overcome "this world." It will be entirely overcome, however, only when we shall have completely crucified our material sense of life and realized the non-existence and non-power of any material sense of self. The first evidence of this new state of consciousness will be a resurrected selfhood. It will be said of us, "He is a better man—or woman—a healthier man, more kindly, more tolerant, more patient, more just." Nevertheless, the wound marks of our old selfhood will still be in evidence. There will be traces of our old human self around until that day of ascension in which we rise so completely above material sense that there will be no evidence of either a physically healthy body or of a physically discordant body.

The first sign of our spiritual development is apparent in the disappearance of the discords and inharmonies in our lives. The next and the higher step is the rising above even the material sense of good into the realization of what health, wealth, and immortality mean when viewed from the standpoint of "My kingdom," the kingdom of God which is within the consciousness of every individual.

In your meditations, there will come from time to time the experience of the risen Christ. You will have a definite and distinct feeling of a Presence greater than yourself but which in reality is your Self—the higher Self with which you are not yet too well acquainted. There will not be two of you, even though there will seem to be two. The real Self will not tarry too long: It will come and it will go. The periods of its absence will be the dark night of the soul—those moments of desolation through which we pass when we realize that we are just human beings and that we have lost contact with that true spiritual being which we know we are and which we long to live and demonstrate and show forth as a light to the world. Therein lies our struggle. We see how far we are from attaining that which we intellectually, and even sometimes spiritually, glimpse. It is a warfare between the Spirit and the flesh. It is a warfare between Christ, our true identity, and that material sense of existence which has been built up in us throughout the ages.

Rising Above Both Discord and Harmony

Wherever Christ is realized within yourself, even if only momentarily glimpsed on a mountain top, you will find that that Christ will draw to you a higher and better human manifestation in the form of health, beauty, wealth, and relationships until that day when material sense will be swallowed up and our spiritual identity be revealed as the all and the only of us.

The first stage of our climb to spiritual heights, the first stage of our discipleship or initiation, is that in which we long to be rid of every physical discord and all mental, moral, and financial lack and limitation. We long to be free of all sense of material discord, little dreaming that what we are praying for is more materiality, only of a better nature. We are already experiencing a measure of good in our lives but we would like to have it increased fourfold or tenfold. We measure that good by human standards: We want a heart that beats normally according to medical standards. We want the liver and lungs to function in accordance with what we call normalcy. We want an income which, according to world standards, is abundant.

The fact that we do attain some measure of health, harmony of human relationships, or abundance of supply as the first fruits of our search for God is probably what keeps us on the path, but to many of us it is a stumbling block because it permits us to tarry in the satisfaction of what we have attained.

That must not happen to the serious student of The Infinite Way. If the discords and the limitations of life, if the sins and inequalities of life are disappearing in some measure from your experience, do not rejoice overly much at this evidence of greater physical, mental, moral, and financial harmony. These are only beginners' footsteps leading to the overcoming of material sense in which even material harmonies disappear, and "My kingdom," the spiritual kingdom, is revealed.

People ask now, just as in the days of the Master, "Where is this spiritual kingdom? How do I recognize it and how do I attain it?" The answer today must be the same as when the Master told the seekers of old, "Neither shall they say, Lo here! or, lo there! for, behold, the kingdom of God is within you."[1] This kingdom cannot be seen with the eyes. No

[1] Luke 17:21.

one can recognize it through material sight. The Messiah comes only to the consciousness of those who recognize and realize Its possibility and, in addition, have the necessary passion for Its attainment. Be assured of this: There is a passion necessary for it today just as in the days when the early Christians were willing to suffer imprisonment, to be thrown into lions' cages, to be crucified on the cross, or to be burned at the stake.

The attainment of the Christ is not a simple achievement in this day and age any more than it was when the Master said that the way is straight and narrow, and few there be that enter. Ultimately, everyone must face within himself the crucifixion of the material sense of existence so that there may be a resurrection and an ascension. The opposition which we encounter in the beginning of our spiritual ascent we nearly always ascribe to others. We believe that others are battling us, but that is not correct. In each of us there is still some measure of material sense, and it is that material sense, deeply embedded in our consciousness, which causes the conflict.

There is an area within each one of us that is never penetrated by anyone. That area within ourselves is where our battles must be fought and where the overcoming must take place. We do not have to overcome people; we do not have to overcome governments; we do not have to overcome ideologies. We have only to overcome the material sense which still exists within ourselves, and the degree of the battle, the nature of the battle is determined by the tenacity of some phase of material sense which exists within us.

Trials and tribulations compel us to surrender human peace and material good for spiritual awareness. It is only through the severest problems that the highest rising in Spirit takes place.

* * *

EASTER[1]

In the Christian world, the Easter season is celebrated in remembrance of the Crucifixion, Resurrection, and Ascension of Christ Jesus nearly 2,000 years ago. According to Christian teaching, the Master submitted to the Crucifixion in order to prove the rightness of his teaching and to demonstrate his ability, even though his body were destroyed, to rise up again in three days. It is taught that by submitting himself to the death of the body, he took upon himself the sins of the world and, thereby, died for our sakes.

Easter, then, is a commemorating of these events—an honoring and a remembering of the man who willingly went through this experience for the sake of the world. The truth-student can unite with the entire Christian world in singing hymns of praise and in paying homage to the one who, out of the magnitude of his love and understanding for God and for man, demonstrated through the Crucifixion the ability to rise from the tomb and to ascend above all human belief. The truth-student likewise understands that in the experience of crucifixion the Master literally demonstrated his power over the evils of enmity and over the material laws of life—

[1] By the author. Reprinted by permission from *The Seeker*, Perth, Western Australia, April, 1957.

laws which, virtually, give the power of life to the body, instead of recognizing that Life, Itself, governs the body. To the truth-student, the Crucifixion also symbolizes the destruction of worldly sin.

The longer one studies the New Testament accounts of the message and the mission of Christ Jesus, which resulted in this series of Easter events, the deeper grows one's love for the Master, and for his work. With this love, there comes a great longing to understand the principle of his life, of his mission, of his message, and of his demonstration. Greater love hath no man than this, that he lay down his life for his friend. What then must be the response within us, as we contemplate the depth of the love which this great soul has given to the world in the demonstration on Calvary and in its culmination in the breakfast by the sea of Galilee and in the Ascension.

When the truth-student becomes sufficiently inspired by reading and by pondering and meditating upon this glorious experience lived by the Master for our sakes, he must then take the next step and ask himself: What is the principle underlying the Crucifixion, Resurrection, and Ascension? What lesson did the Master mean to convey to us? Was the Master telling us that he was undergoing this experience in order to show us that we too may know crucifixion, resurrection, and ascension? Was the Master telling us that this was the demonstration of a principle which we must study, absorb, live, and ultimately demonstrate? Is the Master, in these experiences, presenting to us the principle of immortality, and, if so, what is this principle that is being shown forth in these experiences?

All spiritual seers have learned that every soul born to the earth must undergo the same crucifixion, resurrection, and ascension as shown forth by Christ Jesus, and they have embarked upon the mission of learning the principles involved, living them, and then demonstrating them for the benefit of others. No one may rightly become a practitioner or teacher of spiritual truth until, in some measure, he has undergone the experience of crucifixion and resurrection and has finally turned his steps in the direction of the demonstation of the ascension. No truth-student may hope to experience spiritual health, supply, home, or harmony in human affairs, until he, too, in a measure, begins the study, practice, and demonstration of the principles behind the events of the Easter season.

Our crucifixion begins the moment we accept the Christian teaching that "I can of mine own self do nothing[1] . . . the Father that dwelleth in me, he doeth the works."[2] Right here is the beginning of our release from personal effort. It is our recognition that man shall not live by bread alone, that is, by physical powers or physical efforts or even by human wisdom, but rather that life is sustained by every word that proceedeth out of the mouth of God. Here we learn our first lesson in spiritual healing, which is that life is not dependent upon the action of the heart or other organs or functions of the human body, but rather that the activity of the functions and organs of the human body are dependent upon our consciousness of spiritual truth.

It is essential that we do not hasten past this

[1] John 5:30. [2] John 14:10.

unfoldment until we have thoroughly learned that our health, our supply, and the harmony of our human relationships are not dependent on human effort alone or human wisdom alone or on physical power, as we have believed because of our experience in the human scene; but rather that every word of God, entertained in our consciousness, eventually becomes the harmony of our daily experience. Now we learn the true meaning of Jesus' words, "I have meat to eat that ye know not of."[1] Understanding the word of God, and abiding in this Word and letting this Word abide in us, we have an inner substance, an inner source of good, an inner healer and saviour—the meat that the world knows not of.

We crucify human fears and doubts when, instead of rushing about madly and, with worry and concern, undertaking the tasks of each day, we can relax in the realization: "I am the bread and the wine and the water. All those things the world feverishly seeks through anxious thought and much physical labor are already mine." We relax in God's assurance, "Son, thou art ever with me, and all that I have is thine."[2] Here too, is crucifixion in another form, the crucifixion of unrest, distrust, and burdensome labor.

Pondering the Master's message of forgiveness so often repeated in the Gospels—the message of forgiving "seventy times seven" all those who abuse us, and forgiving even to the extent of praying for those who persecute us and deal unjustly with us—we further learn that, in the degree in which we put this message into practice, do we crucify our hate, prejudice, bigotry, and our fear of our fellow-man.

[1] John 4:32. [2] Luke 15:31.

Meditating deeply upon the message of the Master, which reveals that it was his mission, the Christ-mission, to heal the sick, raise the dead, open the eyes of the blind, and open the ears of the deaf, we realize that this He, who says, "I will never leave thee, nor forsake thee.[1] . . . I am with you alway, even unto the end of the world,"[2] this He is the Christ, ever present with us, performing Its same mission now as of old, healing our minds and bodies, purifying our souls, forgiving our sins, feeding us with the bread of life, and sustaining us with the water of life eternal. And so once more another part of us is crucified.

The culmination of this experience of crucifixion comes into your life and mine through the constant study and practice of a spiritual message until one beautiful day the truth dawns in our consciousness, "Know ye not ye are the sons of the living God." Then all personal sense within us has been crucified and is dead. It takes but a short while, symbolically called three days in the tomb, for the realization to dawn upon us that we have been reborn, and this time, reborn of the Spirit. In this realization, we, too, step out of the tomb—the tomb of human belief, the tomb of physical powers, the tomb of human personality. As we reveal ourselves to the world, we show forth more and more of the qualities of divine sonship; but in the early stages of this rebirth, just as the Master still showed forth the body with the marks of the crucifixion on it, so do we for a while show forth some of our old human faults, human failings, and human tragedies. These are but

[1] Hebrews 13:5. [2] Matthew 28:21.

the outer appearances remaining with us for yet a little while: Inwardly we have realized the resurrection, the rebirth—the new birth—the divine sonship.

Now we walk the earth as spiritual sons of God, though outwardly appearing in the same human forms and, occasionally, showing forth some of the marks of our past. These, too, remain with us only for what symbolically might be termed the "forty days," but even during that period, we walk the earth, a living evidence to our disciples and to our friends and relatives of the spiritual sonship which we have attained and the fruitage of that attainment.

This is the period when our world begins to perceive that no longer do we depend upon man whose breath is in his nostrils, no longer are we afraid of the Pilates of this world, no longer do we thrill to many of the seeming successes of this world; but rather that we have achieved an inner grace, an inner communion with our Father. Like the Master, we walk up and down the earth in humble confidence, telling the world, "I can of my own self do nothing, the Father within me is doing the work."

While Infinite Way students all over the world realize that they may enjoy healings and other forms of harmony through the experience of practitioners and teachers, and thereby, benefit by the uplifted consciousness of those who have gone a step ahead of them, they also understand that it is necessary for them to learn well the message and mission of Christ Jesus, as given in the four Gospels and in some of the writings of Paul. They understand that it is necessary to study thoroughly this spiritual message so that they, too, may enter into a higher consciousness through the crucifixion of their dependence on human modes and methods—through the crucifixion of their dependence on human might, human wisdom, human powers, and through coming into the actual awareness and demonstration of spiritual power, into the awareness of a life not lived by bread alone, but by every word that proceedeth out of the mouth of God.

Infinite Way students unite with all truth-students in love and deep appreciation for the life and mission of the Master, Christ Jesus, and pray that, in this united consciousness, the grace of God, the Holy Ghost, may descend upon us, that His Spirit may be poured out upon us so that we, too, may go out and comfort the world, heal the sick, preach the gospel to those in spiritual darkness, raise the dead from their tombs of material belief, and thereby earn the ascension above all phases of material sense.

TRAVELOGUE

As I write this Travelogue, which you will read in April, it is January, and we are in the beautiful city of Melbourne, Australia, a city of parks, dotted with magnificent trees and colorful flowers which are at their mid-summer peak of loveliness. We have a closed class of students who have come from considerable distances when measured on the map—Brisbane, Sydney, Adelaide, and, of course, Melbourne, itself. The theme of our work is: Any form of fear is a burning of incense to other gods—atheism, a forsaking of God. Only as that fear is replaced with the conscious realization of one Power can we experience Easter.

Easter—the season dedicated to the Ascension! Is there a secret in the Easter lesson for us to discern? Assuredly there is, since every experience related in the Bible has an esoteric, an inner or hidden meaning, discernible only to those who have eyes to see and ears to hear. Easter commemorates that moment when Jesus was "carried up into heaven."[1] But is it possible for a human being to rise on a cloud—to ascend against the pull of gravity while still carrying his physical weight with him? Certainly it is not possible as long as there is a belief in material force or a belief in the power of matter, and that is the significance of Easter. It symbolizes the Master's rising or ascending above the human sense of life, above all material power.

To believe in the power of material force is atheism. God is Spirit; God is infinite; and therefore, Spirit is the all-power. To place power in matter, in form or effect, is the atheistic belief that denies God *all* power—that denies the infinite nature of Spirit. Fear of material conditions, whether of body or bombs, is a retreat into atheism because it is a denial of God.

An official of the British government, after a tour of the United States, told the English press that the United States is a fear-ridden land. Upon returning from the United States, a minister informed the Australian people on a television broadcast that the amount of fear in America is shocking. Newspaper articles here in Australia report that the President

[1] Luke 24:51.

of the United States has begun a religious campaign in the form of prayers before and after meetings, that the Vice-President is opening his talks across the land with prayers, and that politicians are praying—all this in an America gripped with fear.

These prayers of which we read are not, for the most part, the outgrowth of a deep love of God or an unswerving confidence in God. Rather are they the product of abject fear—the fear of bombs. Certainly if these prayers represented love of God and confidence in His power, there would be no need to frighten the citizens into spending more billions for nuclear weapons.

Students, squarely face and meet all fear here and now. Be not mesmerized into accepting this mass hysteria. Remember the meaning of Easter: the demonstration of the powerlessness of material force. Remember that every spiritual healing you have ever witnessed is proof of God and of the impotence of the power of material force. When tempted to accept the atheistic belief of the invincibility of material might, remember that God alone is power; Spirit alone is substance and law. To give power to the organs or functions of the body, or to bombs, is to worship other gods, other powers: It is burning incense to other gods. All fear is atheism, a denial of the one God, the one Power, the one Being.

The history of the Hebrew people, from their days of slavery under Pharaoh throughout their struggles, as they journeyed from Egypt to the Holy Land and in the Holy Land, over the centuries up to their experiences in the time of the Master, Christ Jesus, is one of strife and struggle, with a few victories but more defeats, with some degree of enlightenment and then more ignorance, superstition, and fear. By the time of the Master, the political life of the Hebrews is under the domination of Caesar and his representatives and their religious life under the domination of self-seeking Hebrew leaders. After centuries of such strife and discord, it is not unnatural that crucifixion should be a normal part of existence.

Crucifixion, however, belongs to those ancient Hebraic days and for us today represents our struggle out of human sense. That intermediate period in our unfoldment when the Christ has touched our consciousness and when we have become alive to the possibilities of rising out of the tomb of discordant and inharmonious physical life is the resurrection. When the Christ, the Spirit of God, is come to us, when the Christ is in the ascendency in our consciousness, we approach the ascension; and then it is that we enter a state of consciousness in which crucifixion and resurrection pass from thought, never again to be remembered. This new and higher consciousness, this realm of the reborn, is a life by grace.

If it has been necessary for you or for me to live through those Hebraic days of trial and tribulation, sin, disease, and death, and if it has been necessary for you or for me to be crucified in order to experience a resurrection into a new experience, at least we can understand these experiences to be only forerunners of the ascension and a life by grace, and we can quickly drop the past and any remembrance of both the crucifixion and the resurrection.

By beginning at once to teach our children to live

by grace, we can save them the experience of crucifixion and resurrection. Personally, I am convinced that the Master, Christ Jesus, did not intend to perpetuate the crucifixion or the resurrection in our experience, but rather that he submitted to these to prove to us that there is, in the ascended consciousness, a life by grace which, when understood, delivers us and all those who come after us from crucifixion and resurrection.

The grace of God is not a future event, nor is it something which must be earned or deserved. The grace of God is omnipresent. Our work is not to bring God's grace to us, but rather to realize grace through the activity of the Christ in human consciousness.

Looking at a tree, clad in the full glory of its verdure, we are struck with its aliveness. That aliveness has nothing to do with the future or with the past, nor yet with anything the tree has done. Life animates the tree—it is a state of *is*. So with us. We are alive, intelligent, engaged in spiritual activity, about our Father's business, but this is true only because of the grace of God. As soon as we recognize that fact, we are already under the grace of God, and the grace of God becomes a realized experience. If we are expecting to enjoy the grace of God at some future time or if we hope we can do something to bring it to us, it will forever elude us. The grace of God provides whatever is necessary to the fulfillment of this moment. It is maintaining and sustaining us, supporting us, and acting as a unifying cement establishing peace between us and our neighbor. The grace of God is an ever present experience. It was present even before we embarked on the spiritual path. It has even put us on the spiritual path. The fact that we are on this path now is evidence that the grace of God has been operating in our experience to bring us to this place of realization. The grace of God is an omnipresence which is filling us and fulfilling us.

The world cheats itself of the grace of God by thinking of it as a future event. Right here and now, it is grace and grace alone which keeps the wheels in motion. The physical eyes cannot see, nor can the physical ears hear, but the grace of God enables us both to see and to hear. The grace of God never makes a sick human being well, nor a poor one rich, but rather causes the human sense of self to fade as the Christ-Self is revealed. There must be a constant recognition that the grace of God is continuously operating, and then you will know that, because of the grace of God, you cannot fail. You do not get the grace of God: You realize the grace of God.

God cannot be influenced by man to do man's will. God already is doing that which it is God's function to be doing. God cannot be influenced to bless you or me, or yours or mine. God's grace is functioning now in the experience of every individual who opens his consciousness to that fact. In such recognition, how foolish it would be to reach out to God or to expect to have God answer your prayer for what you think you or someone else may need. Since the grace of God is closer than breathing, it does not have to be struggled for but merely recognized, and now prayer becomes a resting in God, a letting, a communion.

The lily is in full possession of God's grace without

any effort or attempt to secure the glory which it has by virtue of its being. God is infinite intelligence, all-knowing. God is divine love, all-supporting and self-maintaining. Therefore, there should be no effort to influence God, but merely the opportunity provided to sit in peace and quietness and let the divine Presence envelop and enfold us.

When *Practicing the Presence* was published in 1955 in England, it soon proved that it was a helpful means of opening consciousness to this life by grace. It showed that by constantly and consciously practicing the presence of God in every experience of our daily life the struggles of existence passed from us and harmony became established in every department of our lives. This book and then *The Art of Meditation* began a new era in the message of The Infinite Way since these took from us much of the struggle to attain and revealed to us more of spiritual harmony through grace.

This month, Harper & Brothers, the New York publishers who first brought out *The Art of Meditation,* will release a revised and enlarged edition of *Practicing the Presence,* and even those of you who have this book in its British edition will find in this latest edition a new book, a higher unfoldment, and, with the new chapters, a whole new experience.

It is my hope now that much of the crucifixion and even the resurrection, which we have heretofore experienced in our metaphysical way of life, may be eliminated, and that through the art of meditation and the practicing of the presence of God we shall be enabled to make the transition from humanhood to Christhood without crucifixion.

You will find that the Christ is come to dissolve all material existence, not to improve it, and that this dissolving of human experience is not a death, is not a crucifixion, but rather a transitional experience through enlightenment, an enlightenment which comes only through constantly living, moving, and having our being in God-consciousness.

These last two years have shown that when students without a metaphysical background find *Practicing the Presence* and *The Art of Meditation,* they are led out of their human discords and strifes without the degree of struggle that many experienced in the old metaphysics.

I know that a new day is being ushered in, and that day is one of a life by grace attained through the conscientious and constant practicing of the presence of God, along with the living of the life of daily meditation.

CHAPTER FIVE: MAY

THE OBJECT OF OUR SEARCH

God does not enter the affairs of men except through individual consciousness. As we open our consciousness to the activity of God, the sleeping Christ within is gradually awakened until there is a point of transition in which the Christ takes over completely. From that moment, we live in the atmosphere of God: God is now living our life.

Until that transition has been made, however, the responsibility is upon our shoulders. Even though the presence and activity of God have been brought into our experience to such an extent that there are miracle-healings, that does not always mean that there will be no further discords and that we shall have complete harmony forever.

In the early stages of our student days, or discipleship, when we begin to enjoy the blessings which are the fruits of the Spirit, there is often a tendency to revert to our human mode of living: We become enmeshed in human concerns and anxieties, engrossed in human pleasures, and thereby shut ourselves off from the activity of God, until, in some trying moment, we reach out and re-establish that contact. We have not become sufficiently stablized in the consciousness of God to remain steadfast in it, but return again and again to our human ways of living and thinking. This swinging of the pendulum backward and forward continues until, sooner or later, we awaken to the fact that we have been see-sawing between Spirit and "this world," experiencing healings followed by discords and then more healings and more discords. This finally leads to a realization of the need for a more consistent pre-occupation with the things of God and the necessity of daily meditation.

As we continue along the spiritual path, we find that instead of giving thirty minutes a day to the realization of God, eventually we are dwelling in God for four, five, and six hours of the day, and experiencing the fruits of the Spirit in the form of greater harmony and less discord. After weeks and months of this practicing of the Presence, God, the Christ or spiritual Truth, begins to become active in us seven, eight, nine, or ten hours out of the twenty-four. By that time, we are at a point where the balance swings over to the other side of the scale: *It* takes over. We do not have to think about making conscious contact with It; It has made contact with us and It maintains Itself as our consciousness. Everything we do is spontaneous because it is Its action expressed in and through us.

In that state of consciousness, the evils of the earth—the snare of the fowler, the pit, the fall—do not come nigh our dwelling place. They do come nigh our dwelling place, however, until and unless God has been made the activity of our individual consciousness, and the Christ has become the animating principle of our being. Then we find that heaven and earth are one; the harmony of heaven has become the harmony of earth.

Often the question is asked, "Why does the Master say, 'Ask, and it shall be given you'?[1] I have been asking all my life and have not yet received an answer?" Why have people for thousands of years been asking God for safety, security, health, peace, and protection and not receiving them? Why is it that people, righteous people, people who go to church, once, twice, three times a week to ask for new automobiles, new houses, new marriages, new divorces, and all the rest of the things of this world, do not receive them? The answer is, "Ye ask amiss."[2] God is a Spirit, and when Jesus said, "Ask, and it shall be given you," he expected, we may assume, that his statement would be interpreted in the light of his teaching. And what was that teaching? God is Spirit. What, then, can we ask of a God who is Spirit except those things that are spiritual?

"The effectual fervent prayer of a righteous man availeth much."[3] What is a righteous man? Many look upon a righteous man as one who is fulfilling human concepts of righteousness, but is that God's interpretation of righteousness? No, a righteous man is that man who is living in accord with spiritual vision, who governs his affairs according to spiritual wisdom. Going to church seven times a week has nothing to do with being spiritual. A person may attend church seven times a week and may still have his attention focused on material things, desiring bigger and better forms of material living. In other words, it is possible to go to church seventy times a week and still be looking for more fish for our nets,

[1] Matthew 7:7. [2] James 4:3. [3] James 5:16.

larger fish, or a better quality of fish, whereas spirituality consists of leaving our nets, leaving our dependence on the ordinary forms and modes of activity.

Righteousness, in the spiritual sense, is a reliance upon the Infinite Invisible. The rightous man does not fight, but stands still and sees the salvation of the Lord. To the world that would be a "do-nothing" attitude, but it would be far from doing nothing. It would be doing that which is almost impossible for most human beings to do. It would be waiting upon the Lord, resting in His word.

The righteous man, according to spiritual standards, could give to, share with, and even receive from any person and yet not be looking to that person for anything. He might have millions of dollars in securities and never once have the thought that these were his supply. He would always remember that Spirit is his source, his substance, and his reliance. The spiritually righteous man may have all the good things of life, enjoy them, and yet not be concerned tomorrow if they should no longer be a part of his experience. Of such a man James spoke truly when he said that the "prayer of a righteous man availeth much."

The spiritual prayer is complete silence: It is a refraining from desire, from seeking, from words and thoughts. It is a state of receptivity, a quiet listening. Nothing in the world of effect is sought after; nothing in the world of effect is desired. There is only one desire—to experience union with God, to have an awareness of oneness.

To desire union with God because of something to

be achieved—with some object in mind—is to meet with defeat. Such an attitude makes God a means to an end. It is an impossibility to use God as a means of achieving something: God Itself is the object of our desire, our prayer, our meditation, our communion—not God for some reason, not God for some purpose, but only God.

To attain God is to attain all there is in life: There is nothing beyond that. There can be no permanent joy in anything of a material nature, but once God has been realized, there is fulfillment on every level of consciousness. As a matter of fact, in attaining God, we go a step beyond health and wealth because in God there is no such thing as health or wealth: There is only the infinity of harmony. There is no sense of lack of any nature; there is no sense of anything to be attained. There is a state of Self-completeness.

Nowhere in Scripture does it state that God will provide a fortress for us. Scripture emphasizes that God is:

> The Lord is my rock, and my fortress, and my deliverer;
> The God of my rock; in him will I trust: he is my shield, and the horn of my salvation, my high tower, and my refuge, my saviour . . .
>
> II Samuel 22:2, 3

> Lord, thou hast been our dwelling place in all generations.
>
> Psalm 90:1

For thou hast been a shelter for me, and a strong tower from the enemy.

I will abide in thy tabernacle for ever: I will trust in the covert of thy wings.

Psalm 61:3, 4

The Lord is my light and my salvation; whom shall I fear? the Lord is the strength of my life; of whom shall I be afraid?

Psalm 27:1

God is life; God is a fortress; God is a high tower; God is the rock; God is the house; God is the salvation. God does not provide these things because there is nothing beyond God. There is not God *and* something for God to provide. God is Itself the all and everything of being, and, in attaining God, there is nothing left to attain, not even health or wealth, satisfaction or peace, safety or security.

The End of the Search

When the idea has been ruled out of consciousness that in finding God things will be added and when people come to the realization that in finding God, they will find all things included, then will come the end of the search for God. When the realization comes that God Itself is the object of the search—for no purpose—in that moment comes the realization: "*I* am in the midst of thee; where thou art, *I* am; where *I* am, thou art, for we are one."

There is a peace that passeth understanding. That peace will never be realized by the person who clings to his desires. The peace that passeth understanding only comes with the realization that there is nothing for which to desire or for which to hope. It is a well-known fact that the more we feed the appetite, the greater the appetite grows—whether that appetite is for food or whether it is for money or pleasure—whatever it is, the more we indulge it, the more insistent is the desire. If we could have all our desires fulfilled in this moment, that is, all desires other than the desire for God, only a very few hours would elapse before there would be another desire, and then we would have to set out to attain that particular goal. There is no limit to desire because desire begets desire.

When desire is eliminated—and that does not imply settling back into lifelessness—when desire for the objects of life is surrendered in the realization of God as fulfillment, we are very close to the goal. Our activity expands, instead of contracting, but that increased activity is always accompanied by the peace that passeth understanding. Very often people misunderstand the mystical way of life because they believe it is a life of doing nothing or accomplishing nothing, sitting on a mountain top or by the seaside, dawdling. On the contrary, to live without desire in the peace that passeth understanding brings such an abundance of activity as eventually leads one to say, "I don't even have time to get it all done." There are no unfulfilled desires; there is no stress; there is no straining after something: Everything is accomplished in and with and through an inner peace. Life has become a glorious adventure.

If, when we are alone, we could find a moment to put all our human cares out of our thought in some such way as this: "Yes, I can truthfully say that at this moment I shall be satisfied if I achieve the realization of God. I am perfectly willing to let the next hour take care of itself if, in this moment, I can attain that peace which passeth understanding—if I can attain the realization of God, without any motive, without any object, without any desire, just the one desire of sitting here this next five minutes or this next hour seated right in the heart of God." Whether or not the experience of God would come at that very instant, we may be certain that eventually it will come. Furthermore, if we persisted in that attitude for a few minutes each day, that peace would descend, and we would find ourselves wrapped in God, enfolded in God, even though it might only be of a moment's or two or three moment's duration. Continuing in that practice, however, would lead to that transition in consciousness in which the Christ takes over our life. Then, from there on, every bit of work given us to do would be done as if God were doing it. It would never be done with desire, ambition, or hope of recognition. It would merely be done through us as instruments of God.

Each one of us must have periods for the realization of the Christ, periods in which we turn to God with no object, with no desire to attain anything for ourselves—not even a healing. There must be no object whatsoever except attaining the realization of the activity of the Christ, no praying even for our friends or neighbors or for the world. If we hear the voice or feel the touch or receive some awareness that the presence and activity of the Christ are with us, where could we go during the day or night that we would not be a blessing to everyone we meet, that is, to everyone who is at all receptive to spiritual things? If, without having any purpose in mind, we set out to attain the conscious realization of the presence and power of the Christ, we would have that which would be fulfillment, not only to our experience, but to all who touch the hem of the Robe, whether or not we even know that they have touched the hem.

God Itself is the object of our search. We have no need of the activity of the Christ in order to direct It to do something for us: *We only have need of the activity of the Christ.* It, Itself, will do all the doing. It, Itself, will be a light unto our feet; It, Itself, will be the salvation unto our souls; It, Itself, will be the multiplier of loaves and fishes. But for us to desire the Christ for the purpose of multiplying loaves and fishes would be to lose It and to insure defeat at the outset. Too many people who think they are seeking God are not seeking God at all: They are seeking health or wealth, and that is why they cannot find God. We usually find what we seek. If we seek health with sufficient persistence, even without God, we shall probably find it, that is, we shall find a physical sense of health. Seeking God must be a seeking of God, and only God—not seeking God *and* something, and not seeking God *for* something.

Spiritual Fulfillment

Try to imagine what would happen if you, at this very moment, could feel within you or beside you the very presence and power of the Christ, if, at this moment, the Finger should touch you and say,

"Here *I* am," or if you could see the Smile looking up at you and saying, "Where do you think *I* have been all this time? *I* am beside you. *I* am within you. Whithersoever thou goest, *I* go. *I* will never leave you nor forsake you. *I* am the Presence that goes before you to make the crooked places straight."

It would be an utter impossibility for you to experience God's presence and not have somebody during the day feel that he was benefited just by being in your presence. It cannot be otherwise because "where the Spirit of the Lord is, there is liberty."[1] Wherever the Spirit of the Lord is, wherever the conscious presence of God is, there is freedom, a spiritual freedom which to our sense interprets Itself as freedom from sin, disease, death, lack and limitation.

Watch the rest that comes to you, both mental and physical, when you achieve the realization of the Presence: You will begin to understand why the Master could say, "I have overcome the world."[2] There was nothing that could come nigh that state of realized Christ-consciousness. Watch the miracle —the weight that drops off your shoulders, the tension that falls away—the very minute the presence of the Spirit is realized. Then you will know what it means to "take no thought"; you will not have anything about which to take anxious thought: You will have only a rejoicing, a joy, an inner pleasure, and for no particular reason. It is a sense of completeness perfection, a sense of fulfillment. The moment the Spirit touches us, and we have felt Its presence, that is the moment in which our sins

[1] II Corinthians 3:17. [2] John 16:33.

drop away, our sinful desires or our sinful thoughts, our fearful thoughts or doubtful thoughts, or our sickly or painful thoughts—these all drop away with the realization of the Presence.

The realization of the Christ is the *end* of the demonstration, not the beginning. The realization of the Christ is the end of the demonstration because it is the fullness of demonstration itself. There is nothing left for which to hope because now there is only fulfillment.

* * *

GREETINGS, TEEN-AGERS

By a Student

I should like to share with you a wider sense of life and living, which many of us who have now passed your age group have found effective. The beautiful part of this living is that it speaks to all humanity—to every age level, to every situation, to every race—because it contains the truth that has always freed man when he discovered it.

Your time of life is an expansive one. You are pushing out from the center of your being, and there seem to be barriers on all sides. Your thoughts and actions oftentimes run counter to the standard of conduct prescribed by your teachers and parents. Sometimes you find that even your everyday activities are curtailed, and you begin to resent us old-timers. Many times you are impatient with us just as you have felt our impatience with you. But we need to be patient with each other because we need each other.

We need the joy of your youth. The freshness of your outlook can help to dissolve many of the unnecessary restrictions which we have accepted. But you also need us because we can guide that rush of life within you and help to channel it into such form as will produce the best results for you, so that it will not be wasted on little foolish spoutings of energy and thus be dissipated. In such understanding, we shall both begin to see that life is not hedged in and restrictive, but is always pulsing forth in the form of new opportunities, new ideas, new ways of living. "Behold, I make all things new."[1]

A completely new relationship with your parents, teachers, and friends will come when you know that all those terrifying feelings of restraint and frustration have only been life pushing itself forth through you and as you. Previously, when someone has said, "Don't do that," it seemed to stop that wonderful surge of life and you resented it and began either to condemn yourself or the person who spoke, silently perhaps, but the magic of just being alive seemed to be shattered.

Now, in this new understanding, all that will be changed. You will begin to see that life is not unlike a relay race. We have carried the torch in the race at full speed up to this point and now we pass it along to you with the unspoken agreement, "Run your fastest; do your best; we are rooting for you while we carry on with other things that we now have to do."

Does this not give you a sense of being a part of the continuity of life? Does it not give you a feeling

[1] Revelation 21:5.

of yourself as an individual with your own particular function to fulfill? Many of the strange new feelings, stirring within you, are because you are entering upon a new phase of living. In *The Art of Meditation,*[1] there is a chapter entitled "The Place Whereon Thou Standest" which will be a valuable aid in helping you discover your particular activity in life. Get to know yourself in the light of this understanding, and your relationship with all those around you will take on a new aspect.

It will also be helpful if, on awakening, you learn to dedicate your day to God; let Him guide you; let Him lead you in the way that you should go; and then start your day's routine. Later on in the day, pause—during the middle of the morning or at the lunch period—and get quiet within for a few seconds. You will find that, as this habit continues, a feeling of comfort, assurance, and well-being begins to grow in you, and that is far more refreshing than a coca cola break. Do this again in the late afternoon and once more before retiring and watch the change in your life.

One word of caution here: Do not make yourself conspicuous during these periods of quiet, but try to be alone if possible for those few minutes of inner quiet. The presence of others and outside noise may at first distract and make it harder for you to become silent. As you continue this program, you will find things working out for you, without fussing and fuming, in a way we call harmonious but which you would probably call "slick." Your friends will

[1] Joel S. Goldsmith. *The Art of Meditation* (New York: Harper and Brothers, 1956), pp. 87-92.

think you have some special "drag" and call you lucky, but you will know that it is appearing like that because you are beginning to work with life instead of "bucking the stream."

Try this out for yourself and see the difference it will make in all your relationships. Things will not "get you down" as they might have done before, because you will be looking at your friends and relatives and all whom you contact throughout the day with different eyes. You, knowing in your heart that you have your own definite function to fulfill, will have no feeling of jealousy or envy of another; such feelings will simply fade away. You will understand too that you do not have to block another because all your needs are met by this life that is within you, even though the need seems to be answered through someone else. This is equally true of all men, women, and children, even if they do not yet realize it.

This attitude will not remove competition from your life, but you will now have a different sense of it. You will still participate in sports, games, and contests, but it will be with a sense of bringing out the best in yourself, not a feeling of "I must beat so and so at this game" or "I must get a dress like Jane's." No, that type of thinking and feeling will begin to drop from you as you become better acquainted with your real Self. You will find yourself becoming more of an individual, not less; more loving, not less; more co-operative, not less; because The Infinite Way is expansive, fulfilling. Life is always sharing, and your circle of life will widen, deepen, and increase. Nothing that anyone does, says, or thinks will take away your joy unless you let it by not being true to your own highest sense of right.

Have faith in your Self, your Self with a capital S, and it will give you a greater understanding and love for all whom you meet and know. In *Practicing the Presence,*[1] you will find a helpful explanation of the meaning of Self, spelled with a capital S. This I urge you to read and study.

As this is being set forth in my den, the sun is rising and beginning to flood the earth with light and warmth which is symbolic of my feelings about your age-group in life—the light and warmth of a new day coming to this old earth.

NOTE TO PARENTS

By a Student

In all your dealings with your child, keep clear and always uppermost in your thought the spiritual identity of your child. When this is the keynote of your relationship, you will have a rock for your foundation. You are guiding him as a parent, grooming him for playing his part in our present social scheme, one that fits into your own family life. But in our highest spiritual awareness, we maintain his integrity, and our own, by always knowing and showing forth that all outer conditions, bodily and social, are in the realm of effect and thereby will always be secondary, never primary. "Is not the life more than meat, and the body than raiment?"[2]

*   *   *

[1] Joel S. Goldsmith. *Practicing the Presence* (New York: Harper and Brothers, 1958), pp. 66-81.

[2] Matthew 6:25.

You already know that my life is one of rich adventure. There are few idle moments and never any dull ones. Sometimes there are painful moments, which may last a day, a night, or even a week, during which a new Christ-idea is being conceived or delivered from me. Always, however, there is the joy and beauty of companionship and friendship wherever I travel.

Replete with such experiences was the trip through Australia, New Zealand, and the Fiji Islands. In Melbourne, Australia, our Infinite Way Class consisted almost entirely of students I had met eighteen months before, and so there was an atmosphere of home and family. In fact, the entire atmosphere of Melbourne is gentleness and beauty. It reminds me of Victoria, British Columbia, in its other world-ness. The hectic age of "tomorrow" has not yet caught up with Melbourne.

From Melbourne, the work took us on to Adelaide in South Australia, where, in the suburbs, you find simple homes and magnificent gardens, small homes set in the midst of beautiful and colorful gardens. The city itself is permeated with indications of a Detroit or Chicago in the making: The machine age is coming rapidly to Adelaide. To my joy and surprise, however, the morning newspaper there devotes its Saturday editorial to a religious article of the most advanced and profound nature. When the time comes that every newspaper features such editorials, the history of the world will be changed.

In Adelaide, what came forth on the subject of

healing is one of the clearest messages of how to heal and how to be healed that has been presented.

We flew across the continent from Adelaide to Perth, on the Swan River, close to the Indian Ocean. Perth is called the Friendly City. It is this and more —a quiet, lovely city out of old England, a city of serenity and peace, but with the outside world pecking at its shell, striving to break in. Here, at the Seekers' Center, lectures and a large closed class were held.

New Zealand was a new country for me, but in Christchurch on the southern island and in Auckland, on the northern island, we found many interested students to welcome us and to hear the message. Both in Australia and New Zealand, the bookstores report that the writings of The Infinite Way are finding a receptive public.

After our lecture and class work we went to the Fiji Islands for a four day vacation and enjoyed the quiet after a strenuous month of travel. Swami Rudrananda of the Ramakrishna Mission invited me to speak to his staff and to 300 of his high school students. This proved to be one of my really great experiences. Imagine talking to a high school student body about God, prayer, and the practicality of religion, and feeling the depth of interest of these teen-agers! After the talk there was tea and then Swami and two of his students invited us to dinner—a real Indian dinner. At one o'clock in the morning, we took off for Hawaii and home. To all those who actively participated in the arrangements for the work in each city of Australia, New Zealand, and the Fiji Islands, words of thanks are inadequate, but deep gratitude is felt for these unforgettable experiences.

Much is happening in The Infinite Way and much more lies ahead of us. In April, Harper and Brothers published an American edition of *Practicing the Presence,* which has been enlarged and revised. A revised edition of *Consciousness Unfolding* in the same format as the new edition of *The Master Speaks* has just been released by L. N. Fowler and Company, Ltd., of London, England. In its March issue, *Triangles,* Tunbridge Wells, Kent, England, printed an excerpt from *The Art of Meditation. The Vision,* published in Kanhangad, Southern India, begins publication of a series of Infinite Way articles, written especially for this magazine. The *Science of Thought Review,* Sussex, England, has an appreciative and laudatory review of the new *Consciousness Unfolding.*

In the past five years I have traveled six times to and across Europe, twice from the north to the south of Africa, twice to Australia, India, China, and Japan. In most places I have lectured and taught and have always had the opportunity of personal talks with people in all facets of religious life. Through newspapers, we are able to read the mind of "this world," the concerns of those people who either have no religious convictions or who have only the orthodox conception of religion with no understanding of spiritual presence and power. Among these people is the torment of fear in these days of nuclear warfare, along with the threatened engulfment of individuality into a slave society under communism or the deadening effect of a socialistic society where everyone is equal, but with the kind of equality of robots. The doubts and fears of "this world" send people into materialistic pleasures and other forms of escapism which dull and deaden the senses.

The world which I meet on my travels is quite different. It is not "this world." My world is among those of religious convictions—the students of metaphysics, the occult, and the mystical. Regardless of the particular facet of religion in which they are seeking for deeper understanding, they are not blind followers of ceremony, rite, ritual, or creed, but are individuals, seeking individually, deeply and seriously, for specific principles of life which reveal eternal harmonies for themselves and for the entire world of men. In these circles, there may be doubts, there may be questions; but there is never fear. Here we find a conviction that there is a spiritual solution to the world's problems, even if this way is not yet being demonstrated to the extent of actually dissolving the ills of mankind. Here the searching goes on with increasing vigor; the hope glows brighter; the devotion grows deeper. That our present understanding and depth of consciousness are sufficient to meet the immediate needs of those on the spiritual path is being proved throughout the world today. This question, however, remains: Are we, the spiritual disciples of the metaphysical and mystical teachings, prepared as was the Hebrew prophet of old to dispel and dissolve material might and temporal power and thereby reveal the power of the living Word?

Clear thinking has proved to all true religious seekers that there is but one problem facing mankind: Will *temporal* power overwhelm the world? All those who seek and find the grace of God know, in their hearts, that spiritual power is the answer to every problem of health, supply, and peace. And so, only one question remains at the moment unanswered: Since all the temporal power threatening the world is but the "arm of flesh,"[1] is there now not a principle or power which can reveal by demonstration the nothingness of material force or power?

"My peace I give unto you: not as the world giveth"[2] but "*My*" peace. Do you know who spoke those words? Do you believe that through God's grace, Jesus of Nazareth could establish you in God's peace? Do you believe this in the past tense—and not in the present? Do you remember the words, "Peace, be still"?[3] Is there any storm this Word will not quiet? Now? Do you recall his gentle call, "Come unto me"?[4] Have you heard him tell Peter, "Put up again thy sword . . . for all they that take the sword shall perish with the sword"?[5]

> I am the vine, ye are the branches. He that abideth in me, and I in him, the same bringeth forth much fruit: for without me ye can do nothing.
>
> If a man abide not in me, he is cast forth as a branch, and is withered; and men gather them, and cast them into the fire, and they are burned.
>
> If ye abide in me, and my words abide in you, ye shall ask what ye will, and it shall be done unto you.

[1] II Chronicles 32:8. [2] John 14:27.
[3] Mark 4:39. [4] Matthew 11:28. [5] Matthew 26:52.

Herein is my Father glorified, that ye bear much fruit; so shall ye be my disciples.

John 15:5-8

Was this true only in the past, or is the Christ a living truth, demonstrable now and always as of old?

As in the days of Christ Jesus, today the world is faced with a choice: On one side are all the temporal power and material force of Caesar; on the other is the "still small voice"[1] calling "come unto me"[2] and be saved; on one side the sword, and on the other the armor of Spirit. "Choose you"[3] resounds through every land. Will you trust material power or spiritual Presence? Shall we meet Goliath with a battering ram—or a pebble? This is a time for decision: "Choose you." On one side is the mass hysteria of fear; on the other, the inner stillness and peace in the assurance that "I will never leave thee . . .[4] I am with you alway even unto the end of the world."[5] Goliath challenges. Is there a David?

[1] I Kings 19:12. [2] Matthew 11:28.
[3] Joshua 24:15. [4] Hebrews 13:5. [5] Matthew 28:20.

CHAPTER SIX: JUNE

SECURITY THROUGH GOD-REALIZATION

STUDENTS of The Infinite Way often ask if there is any specific daily prayer, treatment, or protective work in which they should engage. If they will remember that nothing takes place except as the activity of consciousness, they will understand the importance of a daily, specific practice which may be termed "knowing the truth." Unless students consciously know the truth, that is, the correct letter of truth, they will never attain the spirit or consciousness of truth.

The Infinite Way is an absolute principle, but The Infinite Way does not close its eyes to the discords and errors of this world. It looks fearlessly at error and realizes that it comes from its father, the devil—hypnotism, illusion, nothingness. One of the most important subjects in our entire work is understanding the nature of error—not looking to find some physical, emotional, or mental cause for disease, but knowing the *nature* of error, that is, the understanding of what lies behind error.

Never for a moment believe that you can arrive at a state where you can ignore error. You must learn to face the situation which confronts you and, in facing it, realize the nature, not only of the specific error with which you are dealing, but the nature of all error, which is nothing more nor less than that ancient knowledge of the tree of good and evil. To the person of spiritual perception, good and evil do not exist as powers in the world—not in men or in conditions. Begin to sit down quietly each day until you can bring yourself to a realization that there is now no condemnation to anything in this world. Through this process of meditation, cogitation, and contemplation, eventually you will come to see that God is all, and this will be not merely a statement but a realization: "Ye shall know the truth, and the truth shall make you free."[1]

Whether you are faced with sin, disease, poverty, lack, or limitation, whether you are faced with an overwhelming enemy—regardless of what it is—you must learn that the nature of error is nothingness: It is the "arm of flesh";[2] it is an appearance; it is temptation—anything you want to call it—but it is not power and it has no law to sustain it. It has no cause. That which Scripture calls evil, devil, or Satan is the unillumined mind of man, appearing as minds, forms, conceptions, and opinions: These constitute the world of mind—the world of human creation. From this unillumined mind of man come the changing world pictures—philosophies, traditions, religions, social orders, and theories of government.

Mind Is an Instrument

There is nothing in this world too good for you or for me if we turn to the Father within and let it unfold. You do not have to create your good: You have only to become aware of it. Let your mind

[1] John 8:32. [2] II Chronicles 32:8.

become illumined with truth and thus be an instrument for the awareness of God's infinity pouring through your individual consciousness. Do not try to manipulate the human scene. Do not try to manipulate God through prayer to make Him produce for you what you decide you want and then, in the same breath, call God the all-knowing mind and the divine love that knows your needs. If you have a God who is love, abide in that realization and let the love flow. If you have a God who is infinite intelligence, trust It, first of all, to know your needs, and secondly, to have the power to supply your needs.

The mind which was in Christ Jesus is your mind and my mind in the degree in which it is illumined with a knowledge of truth. Every one of us has the mind which was in Christ Jesus, but not one of us has as yet attained a sufficient depth of realization of it. We think we have a mind of our own and we come under the limitations which inevitably follow, believing that our capacity is limited by the circumstances of birth. Our mind, when illumined, is that mind which was in Christ Jesus, the same mind as the mind of every sage and seer throughout all time and from now unto eternity. Acknowledge that the mind which was in Christ Jesus is your mind and then, instead of doing your own thinking and planning, let the divine Wisdom become your mind, doing it for you, uttering Itself to you, expressing Itself within you, and speaking to you.

The mind is not a creative faculty: The mind is an avenue of awareness; it is an instrument provided for us by which we can recognize and acknowledge that which is. The mind was not given to us for the purpose of creating something, but as an instrument by which we can become aware of the wonders and glories of this universe. My mind cannot create a person, but through my mind I can become aware of his presence. Through the mind, I can become aware of the word of God as it pulses through me; I can become aware of a message from God and repeat it to you, but I cannot create it. My mind is the same mind that was in Christ Jesus which could do nothing of itself, but which could become aware of that which the Father within was imparting to it. Does this help you to understand that the function of the mind is to become aware of that which God created in the beginning—not tomorrow, not yesterday, and not today—but in the beginning? In the beginning, God created all that ever was made, and it is here awaiting our recognition and acceptance.

Daily Realization of God's Presence

Our daily work every morning should certainly be a realization of God's presence, because nothing less than a conscious realization of the presence of God is a satisfactory preparation for undertaking the day's activity.

The realization of God's presence is fulfillment: God realized is a law of harmony unto our being; God realized is the success of our day; God realized is the cement of our human relationships, the love between us as we meet upon life's highway. God realized—the presence of God actually felt—is our bread, meat, wine, and water:

*"I have meat the world knows not of." That meat is a conscious realization of the presence of God. *I* have the bread of life, the realization of the Christ. "*I* am the wine"—the source of inspiration.

When I open my eyes in the morning, I have only one desire—to know Thee aright, to know Thee whom to know aright is life eternal. I do not seek life eternal; I seek only Thee because Thou art life eternal. Therefore, I open my eyes to know Thee, to experience Thee, to fill myself full of Thee—not full of supply, not full of companionship, not full of a home, not full of a successful business, but full of Thee, only Thee. If I can feel Thy hand in mine, what else can I want to go with me throughout the day?

Even if I make my bed in hell, it matters not, as long as God is there. There is only one thing which would ever disturb me—and that would disturb me in the valley of the shadow of death; it would disturb me in hell, or in heaven; it would disturb me wherever I am—and that is if this Father within should disappear from my awareness. I cannot get along alone; I cannot do anything alone. It is the Spirit of God in me that is doing the work.

The nature of our daily work is to bring us to a point of conscious awareness of God's presence. In the beginning, those of you who are young in the work may find that you cannot achieve this awareness before you have to go about your business or household tasks. Therefore, it will be necessary for you to take advantage of every opportunity there is during the day and night to return to silence and introspection, or what we call contemplative meditation, until that "click" comes. When you do attain the ability to meditate and feel the presence of God, then resolve never to leave your home in the morning for business or to undertake your household duties or family responsibilities or to do anything until you have felt that touch, until you have the awareness, "Go ahead, *I* am with you." Then go out and do whatever has to be done, and it will be done successfully because *I* within you will do it through you:

> God is the activity of my day: God is the activity of my work; and therefore, it is God, the infinite Wisdom, which is outlining my day's program. . . . All my good flows from the within to the without. The kingdom of God, of wholeness or harmony, is within me; and in the degree of my understanding of that, I can multiply loaves and fishes for all those who are not yet aware of the fact that they also are a law of multiplication. I realize, also, that because God is infinite, my being is infinite, since I and the Father are one. Therefore, in this infinity of being, I include all of God's good, and because of that infinity, there is no room for error or evil or negation of any sort. Therefore, there are no laws to act upon me.
>
> God is the law unto my being; God is the divine principle of my being; and therefore, that law is a law unto my universe. Nothing outside of me, whether of the past, the present, or the future, can act upon me as law, even for good. Nothing

existing in the realm of effect can act upon me or upon my affairs as law, since God is the only law-giver. God, the divine Consciousness of my being, the very Soul of me, is the only law unto my experience. Therefore, regardless of what the world may call the law of cause and effect, the law of karma; regardless of what the world may call the law of the stars and the planets; none of that is law unto my being, either for good or evil, since my good is derived from the infinity of my own being, which is God. . . .

I know that this power of love, which is God, is a law of attraction, and therefore, it can only attract to me those whom I can love, and those who can love me; those whom I can serve, and those who can serve me; since we are one in Christ. Because God is a universal law of love, only love is expressing through everyone on earth. Therefore, all men, all men throughout the world, not only throughout this world, but throughout what we call the world of those who have passed on, and the world of those who have not yet been born—all those become a law of love and of life unto my being.[1]

If you have to go before a judge, wait until a question is asked and He will answer the question for you. If you have merchandise to sell—regardless of what you have to do—you will never have any concern about it once you have felt the actual presence and power of God. "He performeth the

[1] From the author's *The Master Speaks* (London, England: L. N. Fowler & Co., Ltd., 1957), pp. 314-316.

thing that is appointed for me[1] . . . The Lord will perfect that which concerneth me."[2] Do not use these quotations as affirmations because that will do you no good.

Do not fall into the habit of merely repeating statements of truth as if they, in and of themselves, will do something for you. They will accomplish nothing except to hypnotize you into believing that you have a God-helper at hand before you have actually had the experience of the Presence. If you can accept Scripture as true, however, and if, in the early morning hours of every day, you can realize that the presence of God is with you and that everything is done by and through God, you will establish yourself in the conscious realization of the presence of God.

There are many ways of accomplishing this. One way is the use of scriptural passages or spiritual or metaphysical writings. Take some inspirational statement into your meditation and ponder it; think of its inner meaning, its deeper meaning. As you contemplate Reality, gradually your thought becomes quiet until it comes almost to a stop, and then in the blink of an eye, you feel that quickening, that deep breath. You feel a Presence or you hear the Word, "Go ahead, *I* am with you. All is well." Then your day is safe; your day is secure, because now anything that is demanded of you will be performed by that *He* or *It*—by the Christ, the Presence and the Power within you.

There are no truer statements in all the world than "I can of mine own self do nothing[3] . . . the Father

[1] Job 23:14. [2] Psalm 138:8. [3] John 5:30.

that dwelleth in me, he doeth the works.[1] . . . the battle is not yours . . . stand ye still, and see the salvation of the Lord."[2] If you should be called upon to move mountains, do not worry about whether you can or cannot accomplish that feat because, if you establish the realization of the Christ, if you feel the actual presence and get that "click," you will not have to move them: You will go there physically and then watch what happens through you and as you.

Those with even a tiny measure of understanding of spiritual law have nothing to fear from human weapons. "No weapon that is formed against thee shall prosper; and every tongue that shall rise against thee in judgment thou shalt condemn,"[3] because God is your life, and you are about the Father's business of life eternal. Not one of the weapons of the world that is formed against you shall prosper. God will never leave you, nor forsake you.

> When thou passest through the waters, *I* will be with thee; and through the rivers, they shall not overflow thee: when thou walkest through the fire, thou shalt not be burned; neither shall the flame kindle upon thee.
>
> Isaiah 43:2

> Fear thou not; for *I* am with thee: be not dismayed; for *I* am thy God: *I* will strengthen thee; yea, *I* will help thee; yea, *I* will uphold thee with the right hand of my righteousness.
>
> Isaiah 41:10

[1] John 14:10. [2] II Chronicles 20:15, 17. [3] Isaiah 54:17.

Whither thou goest, *I* will go.

Ruth 1:16

As students of The Infinite Way, we respond instantly to any call made upon us: If a call is made upon us to go to the home of the sick, we do not ask the nature of the sickness; we do not inquire whether it is infectious or contagious, something of a serious nature or merely a minor ailment. We go, placing our complete reliance on the divine Love which prompts us to answer the call. In the spiritual way of life, we are no longer interested in self-protection, as it is commonly understood. We are not interested in the preservation of our own life because we have come to understand that we have no life of our own: The only life we have is the one universal Life which permeates all of us.

Never is there a separation between God and God's creation. God is the very substance, the very essence, the very life and law of all creation. What we call a material creation is our material sense of creation—the product of mind. God is the only creative principle of the universe; therefore, that which we term matter and which through the five physical senses we see, hear, taste, touch, and smell as matter, is, in its essence, mind about which we entertain a material concept or material view.

Are You Governed by a Consciousness of Truth or by World-Beliefs?

The mesmerism of the world would tend to separate us from our conscious awareness of the presence of God. The radio, headlines in the newspaper, and our neighbor's fears all operate as an unseen, mesmeric influence upon us, and if we are not alert, they will tend to create a sense of separation between us and God. At regular intervals, therefore, we must consciously renew that contact with the Father within. How often it will be necessary for us to renew it will depend upon us and upon the nature of our experiences. If we are encountering many frustrating or disturbing experiences, even such apparently minor ones as missing our bus or misplacing things, we may be sure that we need more frequent and deeper contact with the Source. When we achieve the contact, harmony follows normally and naturally and instead of the bus having just left, it will be pulling in when we reach the station.

People are governed by one of two things: by the activity of truth in their consciousness or by the mesmeric influence of world-beliefs. For example, if there is economic prosperity and they are successful, usually it is due to the world-belief of prosperity; if there is a panic or depression and they suffer from it, it is because they are the victims of the world-belief which they have accepted. In Spirit, there are no depressions. The person who has realized his conscious oneness with God knows nothing of either boom times or depressions. He finds that the manna falls abundantly day by day; his clothing waxes not old; he is renewed day by day in mind, body, and spirit. Wherever he is and under whatever circumstances, as long as he is in God-consciousness, fulfillment is unfolding as his experience.

You will not be concerned with what the world calls good times or bad times if you are governed by the activity of truth in your consciousness. But if you are not governed by the activity of truth, that is, if you are lazy, if you procrastinate, if you refuse to entertain truth consciously day by day—many times a day, you are subject to the mesmeric influences of world-belief, and you will fall prey to any one of the million world-beliefs of sin, sickness, and death that can come nigh your dwelling place. You may be of the eleven thousand who fall at the right hand and at the left unless you are consciously abiding in the truth. If you neglect the opportunity to maintain the activity of truth in consciousness, you are under the influence of anything which may come your way: You are permitting yourself to come under universal beliefs. By your acceptance or rejection of these universal beliefs, you determine what governs your life.

Every experience that comes into your life should come, not by accident, not by influences external to yourself, but by your conscious awareness of the truth. This calls for action on your part. This is not a lazy man's work; this is not work for an indifferent man: This is work only for a person who has persistence and determination. Upon such a man, the beliefs of the world will not operate; rather will his God-given dominion operate upon the world. No one can bring this about for you, but you, yourself.

If you get up in the morning and busy yourself with your human thoughts and plans for the day and your attention is centered on the human preparations for the day—dressing, getting to the office on time, shopping, marketing—do not blame anyone for anything that takes place in your experience because you, yourself, have permitted it by not rejecting the mesmerism of the world. It is possible, however, to reject these world-beliefs: You can be one with God if, upon waking in the morning, you take hold of your thoughts and realize:

> * God is the only influence in my experience. This home in which I dwell is a God-governed household. God is the law unto my household, my family, my body, my business. God is the source of my income. My manna falls day by day, by the grace of God—not by might nor by power, not by the sweat of my brow, but by the grace of God.
>
> World-beliefs are but beliefs, and, therefore, they are not law: They are not cause and they can have no effect. God is my mind—the one and only mind—and nothing comes into my mind: Everything flows out from it; it is not acted upon, but it acts upon the world. I am not a receiving station for men's thoughts: I am a receiving and a distributing station for God's thoughts, God's ideas, and God's power. Nothing flows in *to* me; all thought and all power flow out *from* me.

You are one with God when you consciously make yourself one with God. You have always been one with God—always, all the time—but that oneness must come about as an activity of your consciousness in order to be manifested. Therefore, it is important to remember every day that only that which emanates from God, only that which is from the divine Consciousness of your being, is power, and It alone governs your affairs, your mind, your body, your Soul, your business, your household, your wealth, and your health: That which is termed universal, mortal belief is not law, whether it is some theological belief such as a life-expectancy of three score years and ten or a belief that man must be punished for his sins, or any other kind of theological superstition, medical belief, or belief in the inevitability of the fluctuations of the economic structure.

Inertia versus Conscious Awareness and Positive Conviction

You cannot sit back and listlessly say, "If it is right, it will happen." That is giving inertia full sway. You must know this truth: Whatever is of God is law. If it is not of God, it is not law; it has no power, no cause, and no effect. That is not sitting back with the fatalistic attitude, "Well, I am sure, if that is meant for me, that is the way it will be." The determining factor in your experience is the activity of truth in your consciousness. When no activity of truth is operating in your consciousness, world-belief operates as law. In other words, if your attitude is one of "If—if—if," and the world-belief of influenza is prevalent, there is nothing to prevent your succumbing to that belief because world-belief is operating in your consciousness. Take hold of yourself, day by day, and realize:

> * I am governed by the law of God, the law of truth, by the activity of truth in my consciousness. All power is flowing out *from* me. Therefore, none of these world-beliefs shall come nigh my dwelling place—neither medical beliefs, theological beliefs,

nor economic beliefs. None of these shall come nigh my dwelling place because I live and move and have my being in God. I am a man whose being is in Christ. I am fed by the Christ: I have spiritual meat, spiritual wine, spiritual water, spiritual bread, spiritual resurrection, and spiritual life, truth, and love. These feed, maintain, and sustain me.

If you are not as positive in your acceptance of the truth as is the above statement, then you have operating for you only your own vacillating, fluctuating concepts. There is a law of God. It has never failed. You may have failed it, but it has not failed when faithfully followed. Be assured of this: There is no doubt about spiritual truth; there is no indecision about it, and there is no need for any wavering in thought about it. It is a definite and positive activity of consciousness: Any experience that emanates from God in the midst of us is law and is power. Any experience that is one of the world-beliefs must be recognized as nothingness: It has no power, no cause, no effect, no law, and no continuity.

If you train yourself until you gain a positive conviction of these two points, you will find yourself God-governed; but if you do not do this, you may find yourself governed by every breath that blows about out in the outer world: When there is a fear of war, you will react to that fear; when there is a fear of bombs, you will react to that fear; or when there is a fear of depression, you will react to that fear. But if you have identified yourself with the

Christ, if you are that man whose being is in Christ, who receives all his good in Christ, not from outer circumstances or conditions, then, if the world wants to blow itself up, you may not be able to stop it, but at least you will be of the remnant upon whom the new dispensation will be founded. Probably you cannot prevent a depression in the world, but that does not mean that your own experience will be typical of a depression-economy.

Know this truth: In order to be God-governed, you must be governed by the activity of truth in your consciousness; otherwise, you are governed by every whim and every wind that blows, and by every theory and belief. Maintain the truth of being and let the activity of truth in your consciousness be the only law unto your mind, body, being, household, business, and all your affairs.

At first, you may find that many times a day things come up which will disturb you: You are easily thrown off balance spiritually; you wonder what this is going to do to you, what effect that is going to have on you, or how you will handle the other thing. That is the time to stop whatever you are doing for a second, if only for as long as the blink of an eye, and realize:

> * Wait! I do not live by bread alone; I do not live by the world of effect; so therefore, the world of effect is not acting upon me and it cannot do anything to me. The Cause within me governs every effect. I do not live by the activity of any person, thing, or condition out here. I live by the unfolding of consciousness within my own being.

As many times a day as you come into a situation of puzzlement, retreat into your inner being and realize that truth, and that will re-establish you in the consciousness of truth.

You, yourself, must make the transition from being effect to being cause; you must make the transition from being governed by every form of material belief to being God-governed. Until you are ready to make that transition consciously, you are not yet the child of God and cannot please God; you have not come under the law of God, the beneficence of God, or the protection of the everlasting arms. Only the child of God enjoys the protection of those everlasting arms. And who is the child of God? He in whom the Spirit of God dwells, he in whom the consciousness of truth dwells. Never forget that the scriptural passage about him in whom "the Spirit of God dwelleth,"[1] means that person in whom the consciousness of truth is active.

You remember the disciples' experience at sea, how stormy it was and how fearful they were, and how Jesus said, "It is I; be not afraid."[2] Another time he stood on the prow of the ship and said, "Peace, be still."[3] And what happened to the dangerous waves? They were not there. Is anything dangerous in "*My* presence"? No. That is the secret of spiritual protection. Nothing of an evil nature shall be evil in "*My* presence." And so when people ask, "How can God permit destructive volcanoes, floods, famine, or drought?" the answer is that they never were destructive in "*My* presence." They never were destructive to anybody in the presence of the Christ.

[1] I Corinthians 3:16. [2] John 6:20. [3] Mark 4:39.

For in the time of trouble he shall hide me in his pavilion: in the secret of his tabernacle shall he hide me; he shall set me up upon a rock.

Psalm 27:5

Thou wilt shew me the path of life: in thy presence is fulness of joy; at thy right hand there are pleasures for evermore.

Psalm 16:11

* * *

TRAVELOGUE

After our trip to Australia, New Zealand, and the Fiji Islands, there were three weeks at home in Hawaii before we started on this present trip which is taking us across the mainland and on to England, Scotland, and the Continent. Our first stop on this trek halfway around the world was in San Diego, California, where I had the unexpected and joyous experience of speaking for a Religious Science Church. Oklahoma City was next on our itinerary. There I talked to a group of Infinite Way students in the afternoon and at a public meeting of about 200 people in the evening. It is indeed satisfying to witness the unfoldment of this first Infinite Way lecture-work in Oklahoma. On the following Saturday afternoon and evening, students came from parts of Michigan, Ohio, and Illinois to hear two talks in Toledo, Ohio, at a Unity Church. This was another soul-satisfying experience.

Then came Chicago with two public lectures at Curtiss Hall, followed by a closed class at the Congress Hotel, with mysticism and the mystical way of life as the subject of the class. In the week intervening between the First 1958 Chicago Closed Class and the second class, two talks were given in Indianapolis, sponsored by the Unity Book Shop, and two lectures in Louisville at the Unity Church. And now, April 20, we are back in Chicago for a second class, after which comes New York.

More and more The Infinite Way principles of healing are proving successful, and in my world travels, I learn of other movements dedicated to the ideal and practice of spiritual healing which are making increasing use of the principles given in our writings. Inasmuch as these are spiritual principles whose effectiveness is being proved, it is only right that they be made available to individuals, groups, and organizations dedicated to this work. If for no other reason, therefore, than this, The Infinite Way activity cannot be organized and can never be set apart as a separate institution of any nature. Only through perfect freedom and a complete lack of any organization can the principles revealed in our writings be made available to all who wish to use them and, in this way, be recognized as spiritual principles of such a universal nature that they can never be said to belong to any man, group, corporation, or institution of any name or nature. You can see now why and how I have been guided aright spiritually from the very beginning to protect our work from anything that would give the impression that we are another denomination, sect, or organization claiming any right to a personal message.

Let it always be understood that the name, The Infinite Way, is but the title given to a set of principles of spiritual living and spiritual teaching, and that these principles were a direct unfoldment from Consciousness, Itself—from the heart of the Eternal, or God.

That The Infinite Way is a teaching concerning the mystical or spiritual way of life was made evident in our first Chicago class work of 1958 when the entire subject of the first week of class dealt with the mystical way of life. The recordings of this class will soon be heard in every city and every country where Infinite Way tapes are available,

The meaning of the words "mystic," "mystical," and "mysticism" is not understood and because of this misunderstanding, mysticism is often thought of as something undesirable. One of the reasons for this is that one rather well-known dictionary defines these words as something mysterious, dark, and sometimes evil. Webster's dictionary, however, gives the definition which is understood as being correct according to common usage today as well as in past centuries. A mystical teaching is any teaching that reveals the possibility of receiving direct impartations from God or achieving conscious union with God. This definition accurately describes The Infinite Way, which teaches that through meditation it is possible to reach the kingdom of God within and there commune with God and eventually hear the still small voice. In fact, the entire purpose of the teaching of The Infinite Way is to bring seekers of God back to the original teaching of Jesus Christ and to the teaching of other mystics who have always taught that, since the kingdom of God is within you and me, it is possible through prayer, meditation, and communion to become consciously aware of this divine Presence and to experience this Presence as the very Christ or Son of God within us, actually living our lives for us.

The purpose of the spiritual or mystical way of life is to bring God into our daily experience and thereby assure ourselves of a life lived by God's grace rather than by the sweat of our brow. It is our birthright as children of God to live as heirs of God and to live not by might, nor by power, but by God's Spirit, and to understand that this battle of life is not ours but God's, and that we can stand still and witness the salvation—the experience—of God in our individual affairs. Throughout all ages this has been described as the search for the Holy Grail, the search for God, the search for Truth, or the search for ultimate Reality.

CHAPTER SEVEN: JULY

THERE IS NO POWER IN FEAR

In The Infinite Way, students are taught to make a conscious transition from dependence on the visible and tangible to a radical and complete reliance on the Invisible, until they come to a point where they live through and by the Invisible, by that which cannot be cognized by the physical senses. If this practice is continuous, it is not long before that unknown Invisible becomes tangible and evident as a feeling, as awareness, a presence, which is the "peace, be still"[1] to every fear. Only by removing power from the visible and depending solely on the Infinite Invisible can fear be supplanted with confidence.

Fear grips the world. The health of the world today seems to rest upon the precarious foundation of fear. Health seems to be based not on an understanding of God, but on fear. The entire world is held in bondage to the fear of cancer, the fear of heart disease, the fear of infection, and the fear of contagion. We are warned to have the heart examined periodically, to have the lungs x-rayed at regular intervals, and to have tests to ascertain the presence or absence of cancer.

To live in a state of fear is inevitable in a world that lives primarily from the standpoint of preserving

[1] Mark 4:39.

health or some particular form of wealth. Anything that endangers a person's livelihood engenders fear; anything that endangers a person's heart, lungs, or any organ of his body brings fear; anything that endangers a person's human sense of life arouses fear. This is inevitable as long as these material forms are the gods of the human world. If the object of life is merely to live ten years longer or to have a little less pain, or if the primary purpose of life is to be sure that enough supply comes in every week, then anything which might interfere with the achievement of those ends or make them unattainable would result in fear.

Fear is at the root of most of the troubles of those who seek help. Only a few people turn to a spiritual teaching for the purpose of finding God, only a few. The vast majority of those who come to a work such as ours come because of the desire for better health, greater supply, or more satisfactory human relationships, or because of the longing for peace, safety, and security. It is easy to observe how fear develops when the lack of any of these things becomes evident in a person's experience.

In practically every area of life, fear is the dominating influence. Most of the people of the world are living in fear: Safety and security today are apparently founded on the ability of one nation to make others fear it and upon its own fear of other nations. Most of the decisions that have been made in the world of diplomacy have been motivated by fear. In the field of capital and labor relations, many of the settlements which have been negotiated have had their foundation in fear rather than in justice or equity. In nearly every major conflict, the solution has been based on fear.

Fear is rampant. The world is a world filled with fear. Does the answer to this fear which grips the world lie in material force? Is material power the remedy for the fears of the world? Does the solution lie in creating bigger and more destructive bombs, or can world tensions be resolved at the conference table? Has any real confidence or hope resulted from the many conferences held during the past twenty years? Have they offered any solution to the world's problems? Has any diplomat gone to the conference table with any real hope of arranging even a temporary settlement of world affairs without using fear as the means of achieving his end? Is not the climate of every conference one of fear?

The remedy does not lie in the use of material force. Only to the extent that power is removed from the external world and is recognized as an activity of our own inner being is fear dissipated and will it finally be eliminated. As long as a person's thought is centered on the attainment of health, supply, safety, or security, the possibility of his overcoming fear is not very great. The cause of the fear must be eliminated before the fear itself can be overcome.

If a person is fearful of a heart condition, it is of little help to tell him to stop fearing for his heart or for his life, because the heart has become the symbol of life to him. Before the fear for the heart can be given up, it must be brought to light and become a conviction that the heart is not the source of life. Sometimes fear is quickly overcome in the realization that the heart does not give life, but that it is life which animates the heart; life functions the heart.

In the same way, as long as a person considers money to be the measure of his supply, it would be futile to tell him to stop fearing for his supply. All he has to do is to look at his depleted bank account, and his fear amounts minute by minute. To free him from this fear, it must be made clear to him that money does not constitute supply. Fear is removed from what appears as lack when it is recognized that money, like the heart, is an effect and not a cause, and that supply produces a sufficiency of all the money that may be necessary for any purpose.

Removing Fear

The fears of the human race must be overcome by arriving at some understanding within ourselves as to what constitutes life. By life, do we merely mean the removal of the danger of a bomb? By life, do we mean resting in the fact that at a certain age we shall draw social security? By life, do we mean business as usual regardless of what happens to the rest of the world? Or, by life, do we mean the attainment of a state of consciousness in which we find freedom from the fears which are the scourge of this world?

Freedom from fear is achieved by overcoming the conditions which have produced the fear. Once a person stops fearing for his heart, he begins to enter a higher sense of life. His whole attitude changes when he realizes that his life is not dependent upon his heart. He begins to live without a thought for the condition of his heart, and he then finds that the heart is governed harmoniously by life. In the same way, the moment a person, whether on the lowest level of earning capacity or in the highest ranks of business, begins to perceive that money is not the source of prosperity, but that there is that which guarantees prosperity, irrespective of the currency, life begins to take on a different mode of expression.

The overcoming of sin and disease by removing power from the external form and placing it in the Infinite Invisible has been proved. The healing works bear witness to themselves. A respect for the spiritual way as a solution to the problems of this world has grown up throughout the world because of the healings which have taken place. And how are these healing works accomplished? In one way and in one way only—by removing power from the sin and disease of the world. This is done by being willing to face sin or disease, look at it, touch it, if necessary, just as the Master touched the leper, and realize:

> * Thou hast no power; thou art a nothingness appearing to be something, a nothingness claiming to be something, but actually nothingness—nothingness, because power is in and of God. God is power, and there is no other power. There are not two powers: There are not good powers and evil powers; there are not powers of health and powers of sickness. There is only one power.

Then, when a person comes face to face with any form of disease, he can sit peacefully and quietly with a smile on his face which says far more expressively than words:

* You, there, who pretend to be a power, you who are feared so greatly by men that they are looking around for the mightiest weapons they can find to destroy you—you are not power, and I can smile at you, because there is no "you." There is an effect of some kind, but there is no power in it. The power is *I*, the power within me. God's grace is my sufficiency: I do not need the weapons of the world; I need only spiritual armor, not material armor. I need the sword of the Spirit, not the surgeon's knife. The realization of Thy peace is sufficient unto any and every storm.

I have had the opportunity of working with four different organizations which were involved in capital and labor disputes. In each instance, I was called in when the trouble was at its height, and, from that day to this, there have been no further strikes in these organizations and no settlements achieved by other than peaceful means. No human weapons or threats of any kind were used by any of these four organizations: There was brought into them only a spirit of love and a spirit of trust—not trust in each other, but a trust in Omnipresence—a conviction that there is no power in hatred, greed, or mad ambition, but that all power is in God, and it is futile to look to man whose breath is in his nostrils for justice, equity, or mercy, because these cannot be found in the man of earth. The realization of God in the midst of us—this Presence, this Power—makes of no effect human greed or ambition.

Our work in this area is not a work in which virtues are attributed to capital and vices to labor, or in which virtues are attributed to labor and vices to capital. There is no taking of sides in this work, no mental manipulation: This work is a recognition that ambition, hate, jealousy, envy, and strife are not personal qualities: They are not the exclusive possession of the educated or of the illiterate, of the wealthy or of the poor. These qualities are products of the fleshly mind which may operate through a man or a woman in any station in life.

In the understanding that such activities of the human mind are not power, their powerlessness has been proved in this area in the same way as it has been proved in the sick room. In spiritual healing, where no physical or mental remedy is used, I have never yet witnessed a practitioner suffering from infection, contagion, or any of the ills of his patients. When, through sufficient practice, you come to the realization that in all this universe there is only one power and that that power is within you, you can look at any condition and smile at it. If you have a receptive thought with which to work, you will have a quick healing; if it is not too receptive, it will be a slow healing; and if it is adamant in its materiality, there may be no healing at all.

So far as I know, no one has achieved one hundred percent success in healing work. The Master gave the reason for this in his parable of the sower: There is the soil that is fertile, and from that, rich fruitage comes; there is the soil that is barren, and a few temporary benefits grow out of it; and finally there is the rocky soil in which nothing grows. What we are at a given moment is the result of what we have been. From the moment, however, that we are brought into a spiritual study, the opportunity is given us to turn the rocky soil into barren soil and the barren soil into fertile soil by abiding in the Word and letting the Word abide in us, by abiding in meditation, and by our willingness to spend hours, days, weeks, and months in study, prayer, and good works, putting into practice the things we read. Too many metaphysicians read truth-books and expect that the reading alone will make their demonstration. Occasionally lightning does strike; the exception does occur, but only to prove the rule. Reading is the least part of this work: *Putting into practice individual lessons is the major part of the work.*

Sickness and what the world calls sin have been healed many times through the realization of one power, that is, by not fearing or hating the power of sin or disease. The same realization of one power has often brought harmony into capital and labor relations and led to changes in human relationships. Whatever the nature of the fear or the hate, there is no power in it when we bring to the world our sense of spiritual love. This is not denying that there is hate in the world. It is not denying that there is fear. We do not deny any of these things: We recognize that they have no power to be anything, cause anything, or do anything when the realization of one Power is achieved.

Impersonal and Universal Nature of Fear

Disease in and of itself has no power. It need not be feared. True, to some extent, the fear of disease controls us, but this fear is not your fear or mine. It is a universal fear to which we have become subject.

Fear is a universal state, based on the belief that we have a separate life which can be destroyed. This universal fear which we pick up through the antennas of the mind is what is disturbing us, not the disease. Our fear of the disease or condition, or of what it will do to us, is the frightening factor.

The only way evil can be overcome is in the realization of its nature, knowing that a universal fear is handling the world, even your personal world. It is a *universal* fear, not *your* fear. Do not try to cure your own fear; do not try to cure the fear of your patient. If he wants to fear, encourage him to fear a litttle more. That is the quickest way to prove to him that his fears are powerless. Therefore, do not be concerned about the fears of your patient, but remember that fear is an activity of universal belief. Understand that fear is a universal belief, and then realize that there cannot be two powers: There cannot be power in God and power in fear. In that assurance, let fear try to do its work: Do not try to remove it; do not try to rise above it; do not try to overcome it. Why should you, if, in and of itself, it is nothing, if its only power is the power that you are giving it by accepting the world-belief about it?

There is not a condition that you can encounter in your experience or in the experience of your patients, family, friends, or students—no situation in life—that will not respond to the understanding that underlying the entire situation is fear and the powerlessness of that fear. Fear is universal: the fear of annihilation; the fear of disease because it will lead to death, that is, to the extinction of our life; the fear of lack because we may freeze or starve. Fear grips the world as a universal claim, but *fear is not a power.* The moment you realize that, you have taken the sting out of fear and made it ineffective and inoperative, and you have set yourself, your patient, or your student free in his spiritual identity.

Face Fear and Recognize Its Powerlessness

We need to lose all fear of external power, whether that external power is in germs or in bombs, whether that power is in strikes or in shutdowns, whether that power is in poverty or wealth. We must withdraw power from fear.

If someone tells you, "You are in the grip of fear and you must overcome it," you are only thrown deeper into the abyss of fear. But if someone says to you, "You are in the grip of fear, and that is foolishness because fear has no power; fear is not a thing; fear is not a condition"; then that fear is lifted from you and removed from your experience.

Whether the fear is a fear of disease, fear of old age, fear of unhappiness or loneliness, fear of a calendar, fear of lack, fear of war, fear of a depression, fear of a change of administration, fear of a change in your human situation, or simply fear of the unknown, you, yourself, eventually must come to the realization, "Yes, I admit that I fear change; I fear a change in my finances; I fear a change in my health; I fear a change in my life; I fear the extinction of my sense of life; I fear the death of my body. But despite the fears in my inmost being, I know that fear is not power."

Fear is removed, not by declaring that God is all or that God is love, but by an inner realization that

God alone is the only power, and that fear, whether individual or collective, is not power. Never tell a person who is fearful to stop fearing; never tell him that there is nothing to fear because if he could accept that he would not be fearful. Rather, silently within yourself, smile and realize the nature of fear as powerless—a nothingness.

Minorities fear majorities; majorities fear minorities; and yet actually there is no basis for such fear because minorities and majorities can learn to live together in cooperation. There is no use, however, in telling that to anyone who is fearful of being outnumbered and whose confidence is in numbers. Always a minority has feared being ruled by the majority, and the majority in its turn has not felt comfortable alongside its minority. Minorities have been enslaved because majorities were afraid of having the minority become free.

From the beginning of time, this world has been ruled by fear. Fear has governed the emotions of men, and as long as fear is acknowledged to be a power, that will continue. But it need not continue: You and I can change that. The student of spiritual wisdom can make a beginning in small ways, either in his home or among those who come to him for help. In some way, the fears of the young student must be met before he is ready to seek God or to put forth the necessary effort to live the spiritual life. When a person needs help, he needs help because he is fearful. If he were not fearing, he would not be asking for help. It may not be a conscious fear, but it is fear, nevertheless. Fear is not personal: Fear is a universal claim. Now, this minute, understand that fear, in and of itself, is not a power. Withdraw power from fear, and your realization of your oneness with God, in which the truth of the non-power of fear is recognized, will prove to be a majority.

Most people who study metaphysics do so because of fear. They fear disease; they fear lack; they fear a change; or, they fear loneliness. To tell them this probably will not help them, but you will help them by knowing that the fear which is driving them to truth is not a power. Fear itself is nothing but a universal claim. Realize that neither individual fear nor collective fear is a power: "*I* am power. The power is within me—within my consciousness and yours. The kingdom of God is within me." As you cease giving power to fear, all power disappears from fear, and you have then set yourself or your patient free. Your patient will tell you that he feels happy or at peace, but what he does not realize is that his fear has been taken from him, that is, the power that fear had over him.

Health does not remove fear because the fear of becoming sick or old, or the fear of dying or having an accident still remains. Becoming prosperous is no deterrent to fear because there still remains the fear of losing one's possessions. Gaining high honors does not remove fear because always the fear of losing them at some future time looms. A demonstration of health, prosperity, or fame, in and of itself, will not establish permanent harmony. Unless the destruction of the power of fear accompanies the healing, there will always be the possibility that your patient will become embroiled in something which brings seven times more devils upon him. Healing alone is not enough if the patient still retains his fear. That is one of the mysteries of this work.

Many students enjoy only intervals of health between sicknesses. That is not health; that is not harmony. Our healing work is evidence of what spiritual living can bring. Our work is not in the realm of merely healing sick people and making them well so that they can go out and get sick again or indulge in more dissipation. Our class work, books, and recordings provide opportunities for spiritual enlightenment, and whatever light comes to you will come from your years of devotion to spiritual literature and devotion to prayer and meditation.

When you are engaged in healing work, it is necessary not merely to heal the sick, but to be sure your student or patient is studying so as to learn the true meaning of this work. The young student has not developed the spiritual consciousness requisite to heal himself, so he seeks out one who is dedicating his life to God—to spiritual unfoldment, to the Christ—and because of his contact with that enlightened consciousness, the young student benefits. But that young student, in his turn, must go and do likewise. We are all entitled to the help of one another along the way, but let us at least be making some effort towards gaining spiritual enlightenment.

Our healing works are the signs following. The signs following what? Spiritual consciousness—the development and cultivation of spiritual consciousness. The goal of our work is conscious union with God. The goal of our work is the ability to live and move and have our being in God-consciousness. The healings are the signs following. They will be added unto you *if so be you seek the kingdom of God and His righteousness first. No signs will be given beforehand.*

Let it be very clear that we are not dealing with fear of anything or of anybody. Our concern is only with the word "fear" itself. This fear is a universal fear which in the last analysis is really the fear of self-extinction. That is the basic fear. Beginning with this moment, however, we must give wholehearted acceptance to the truth that fear, in and of itself, is not a power. Fear underlies all our ills and all our troubles, but this is only because we have accepted fear as a power or because we have developed a fear of something or someone to which we have attributed power. Withdraw the power from fear of the condition or the person, and you have met the situation. Not only have you met that particular situation, but through this practice you have spiritualized your consciousness to the extent that never again will you fear quite so deeply—never again will you fear sin, disease, lack, or limitation quite so deeply. Gradually you will find fear playing less and less of a part in your life. Fear is now being replaced with understanding, and it is then that grace takes over.

Release Fear and Live by Grace

Our lives must be lived by grace. Whatever we do, there is a divine power, the power of grace, working within us and through us to the successful conclusion of that undertaking. The government is upon Its shoulders. We work—we do whatever is given us to do in a human way—but it is the power of grace that works through us. The power of grace feeds us and sustains us, and even though we continue to work, we no longer work for a living because now fear is not the motivating force driving us to work. We no longer work for a living: We work because it is an activity of our being—normal, natural, and right.

A musician does not stop being a musician just because it is not necessary for him to earn his living with his music; an artist does not stop being an artist because he is financially independent and does not have to earn a living by practicing his profession. In the same way, we do the work given us to do even though it is no longer essential to our livelihood. We do our work because it is a part of our being, but our living now comes by grace.

Grace, however, cannot work in us or through us while we permit fear of the little "I," this little me, to govern us, or let the fear of losing that little "I's" possessions block the power of grace. When we realize that there is a power of grace functioning in this world bringing our good to us, we begin to lose our fears. God's grace is our sufficiency in all things: It feeds us and clothes us and heals us, maintains us and sustains us, but there is a responsibility that we have to accept, and that responsibility is to become free of fear.

The most difficult thing for most people in this world to believe is that there is a power of grace in this universe which would prevent their ever again having to worry or fear. We cannot become free of fear except in proportion as we realize that there is no power in the external universe. All power is within ourselves acting upon this universe. Nothing from without can enter to defile or make a lie—

nothing from without—because there is no power in anything in the without. The realization of this sets us free and enables the power of grace to operate.

There is a power of grace that will heal us; there is a power of grace that will supply us; there is a power of grace that we can carry into personal, industrial, national, and international relationships. This power of grace operates when fear has been recognized as having no power, being of no power, governing nowhere at any time. Overcome fear by understanding that that which is external is not power, whether it is a person, place, thing, or condition. The presence of the gentle Christ is sufficient to calm the storms of life. Live through the Spirit; turn to the Spirit for everything; react only to the Spirit. Let the Spirit be your law, life, activity, and being.

We have been taught that the moment lack is supplanted by abundance, there is no fear; the moment disease gives way to health, there is nothing left to fear; the moment sin is replaced by virtue, there is no fear. The fact is, however, that the reverse of this is true: Take the sting out of fear, and the lack and the disease will go. There never will be an end to fear by removing some object which is feared because as soon as it is removed another object to be feared even more greatly rears its head. The fear must be removed first, and then the object of the fear disappears. When we no longer fear, there will be no dictators to fear, there will be no economic system which looms as a giant leviathan to be feared: There will be love in the world, a spiritual love based on the fact that there is no other power.

AUTHOR SAYS GOD CAN BE EXPERIENCED

A review of *Practicing the Presence*[1]

Merab Eberle

This is an important book. It speaks with authority in a world given over to mental chaos. Here we may learn how to become acquainted with God and His peace.

Can mankind be delivered from dictatorship, bondage to the ills of the flesh and fears? The author, an internationally recognized spiritual leader, says "Yes." He sets forth in these pages the method he employed to come under the government of God.

He was a frustrated man, a troubled man, Joel S. Goldsmith writes; and it was during one of his periods of contemplation and cogitation that the words came to him, "Thou wilt keep him in perfect peace, whose mind is stayed on thee."[2] This surprised the author because, at that time, he was but little acquainted with the Bible and only occasionally went to church.

Through the study of scripture and the practice of its teachings, the author at length realized that a Presence was with him, counselling, sustaining, leading him on and up into greater spiritual awareness. Since then he has traveled throughout the world and, in lectures and classes, he has taught others to know the Presence.

This experience of God, he writes, can be gained

[1] Reprinted from *The Dayton Journal-Herald*, Dayton, Ohio, April, 1958.

[2] Isaiah 26:3.

by "consciously, daily and hourly, abiding in some great spiritual truth. . . ."

God, to Mr. Goldsmith, is not an order of parent who withholds His good from men until He is beseeched to bestow treasure. Rather, He is the constant Giver, and it is up to the human being, through the process of dying daily, to abide in God and thereby come into the reign of spiritual abundance which supplies all needs.

Mr. Goldsmith indicates that the reason for the world's lack lies in the fact that man does not comprehend what the Master means in his statement ". . . he that hath, to him shall be given: and he that hath not, from him shall be taken even that which he hath."[1] Those who come to know that they live by the boundless grace of God, and so pour out what they have, will find the riches of existence coming in to them. "The cup of joy runs over, and all that the Father has flows forth into expression."

The author makes much of the art of meditation. Indeed, Harper and Brothers published Mr. Goldsmith's *Art of Meditation* last year, a book in which the spiritual student may learn how to meditate rightly. It is when the human mind is stilled through proper meditation, the author writes, that the Presence makes itself manifest.

Some day, after much practice and much meditation, the "Moment of Christhood" will arrive, we are told. Having reached this point, we shall come to know that Christ "is the substance of every experience . . . on the outer plane."

"Seek neither health, nor wealth, nor fame, nor

[1] Mark 4:25.

fortune," the author writes. "Seek first the realization of this inner kingdom and be a beholder as these outer things are added."

Several of Mr. Goldsmith's books have been published in England. These include *Consciousness Unfolding* and *The Master Speaks*. His best known book here and abroad is *The Infinite Way*.

* * *

TRAVELOGUE

An Infinite Way Travelogue does not have too much to do with scenery and countries as such, since the object of my travels is to carry the message of The Infinite Way to human consciousness, wherever there is receptive thought. And so the account of our travels deals chiefly with people—old friends and new—and experiences pertaining to the unfoldment of the message of The Infinite Way here, there, and everywhere. From these travels and experiences, come spiritual unfoldments, and these, too, belong to all our students and, therefore, often find their way into this portion of *The Letter*.

Sometimes, however, I cannot refrain from telling you of experiences with people and about events not directly connected with our spiritual activities: being in Holland two successive years and experiencing the gladness, joy, and beauty of tulip-time there; my first trip to Johannesburg, South Africa, where I almost expected to find the darkest Africa of Dr. Livingstone only to see a city as modern as tomorrow, as colorful as Hawaii, and with a surprising spiritual vitality; or my first view of Victoria Falls, flying low over the Falls and seemingly almost going down into them. Such sights make one exclaim, "It can't be true and it can't be real!" But soon you realize that it is, and grander, too, than any stretch of the imagination.

Looking down from an airplane upon the magnificence, grandeur, and beauty of the Alps Mountains, it is possible to understand more nearly the magnitude of God's work. Witnessing an audience of the Pope in St. Peter's Cathedral in Rome, a man-made spectacle such as only a De Mille could conceive, is another experience which sends me back into consciousness for further light on the activities of the mind of man.

On Mauritius Island, in the Indian Ocean, I have experienced an aloneness such as is impossible for me to describe—as if I were really the only person left on earth on an island far from the knowledge of man. Twice I have stood at the great Castle in Edinburgh, Scotland, and have witnessed the mystical vision of transparency, both of the buildings and of all nature.

Among the highlights of these travels are visits with others on the spiritual path. Such experiences are but the outer expression of consciousness and only demonstrate how they can be enjoyed by all those who set their hearts and souls on the attainment of at least some measure of God-realization. Only in proportion to the development of the spiritual side of our nature are we brought into contact with those engaged in that same spiritual search.

As I re-read the many Travelogues in *The Letters*, I feel very clearly the truth of the theme of *Metaphysical Notes*: "My conscious oneness with God constitutes my oneness with all spiritual being and idea." As we meet Infinite Way students, first in one city and then in another, and often in one country and then another, the universality of this truth is apparent.

Now we are in New York, our work having been completed in San Diego, Oklahoma City, Toledo, Indianapolis, and Chicago. Following the class on "Mysticism" in Chicago, our New York Class presented a great contrast: It was a class of an entirely different nature, yet one which had a profound effect on the students. To continue the work as it unfolded in the recent Chicago and New York classes, in October there will be lecture and class work in Seattle, Washington; lectures in Victoria and Vancouver, Canada; and in November, six lectures and a class in New York City.

During the second week of class in Chicago, Myrtle Dean Clark, President of the Conference of Club Presidents and Program Chairmen, invited me to be the guest of honor at the final meeting of this organization in Fullerton Hall of the Art Institute, where I had the pleasure of speaking to 400 representative club women from metropolitan Chicago and adjoining states. In New York, I had the unprecedented and joyous privilege of talking to my own Masonic Lodge. God is the very life of Masonry, and so The Infinite Way and Masonry are closely related subjects. Another inspiring experience was giving a talk at a Unity Center in New York, an evening rich in friendship and truth.

And now to London town where we are flying tomorrow, May 14, for more lectures and class work.

CHAPTER EIGHT: AUGUST

THE FATHER-CONSCIOUSNESS

ALL the inharmony of human existence arises because of a lack of understanding of our true identity. This has brought about a sense of separation between us and God, which in turn has separated us from our good. This is similar to the situation in which a person might find himself were he the possessor of a substantial bank account, the existence of which he has forgotten, and because of his failure to remember, he thereby suffers from lack. The remembrance of that bank account would eliminate the lack and immediately restore harmony to his financial affairs.

In like manner, a child who, for one reason or another, becomes separated from his parents and is on his own, alone, feels the necessity of shifting for himself and, therefore, puts forth varying degrees of effort to find a place for himself in the world, whereas the rediscovery of his parents and the return to his home would again establish him in his harmony and sense of security.

Such is the story of the prodigal son. The son had everything—a rich father, a good home, and a well-established position in life. Then came the desire to be something of himself, to achieve something of and on his own. Very quickly he used up his substance: The supply that had been stored up for him was depleted because it was not now being renewed. The son no longer had contact with his source—his father's house. At the end of the road, he came to the realization that even his father's servants were far more fortunate than was he, and slowly he began the return to the father's house. But while he was yet a long way off, his father came out to greet him, to re-establish him in his home, in his sonship, in his heirhood, and all was well again.

Humanhood Is a State of Separation from the Father

Such is the story of all human beings. We are all prodigals. What is the fall of man but a sense of separation from God? It is the descent from divine Consciousness to the belief and acceptance of a selfhood apart from God, whereas the return to the Father's house is the remembrance of our selfhood as God's own Self. There is only one Self, and that Self is God, regardless of what you or anyone else may think about it or how it may be misinterpreted. God is the only Self. We, however, in our humanhood, entertain a sense of self called by many names—Elizabeth, Henry, Joel—and, the moment that happens, we have excluded God; and now Elizabeth, Henry, or Joel begins to search around for some means of perpetuating himself. The fear of extinction and the struggle for survival become the motivating force in human experience with aggression and fear the dominant and recurring theme.

And what is the effect of this fear in human experience? It is easy to observe its effects in the animal world. Animals, with their highly developed instincts, sense the presence or absence of fear. As you come into close proximity to an animal, having no fear of him, the animal instinctively loves you and consequently is friendly. But when you come into the presence of that same animal filled with fear, the animal may not only adopt a defensive attitude, but may become so aggressively offensive that he attacks you. Why is that? Because your sense of self has set up in the animal another sense of self, the one antagonistic to the other. On the other hand, when there is an absence of fear, there is unity and love; there is a fellowship between the person and the animal; and all is well.

Much the same thing happens to us in our relationship with each other. When we come together in a fellowship where there are no mental barriers erected to separate us from one another, where no one in the relationship wants anything of anyone else, where no one is seeking to gain or to get anything, there is a oneness, a unity; there are no longer conflicting selfhoods: There is just one Self—a sharing, co-operative, joyous Self. But let someone in that relationship entertain the idea of gaining something from anyone else—getting, achieving, begging, borrowing, stealing—and almost imperceptibly a wall of defense arises which acts as a barrier and results in conflict.

Out of the sense of separateness, arises the whole world of antagonism with everyone striving to protect and perpetuate that false sense of self which he has erected within himself. Not realizing their true nature as consciousness—God-consciousness—people believe that they need money, protection, houses, or land with fences around it. They place their trust in the trappings of material living and set up defenses to protect their possessions. Then, if they lack their particular concept of sufficient possessions, they attempt to gain the sufficiency which they consider requisite to their happiness, first, by trying to earn enough money; but if they find this too difficult, they may go step by step from borrowing to begging and some ultimately even to stealing. Such ill-advised means would be impossible to anyone who is living in the realization that God, individual consciousness, embodies and contains within Itself the infinity of being. There would be no giving of power to things—no seeking or desiring things—because, as things come and go, the realization would always abide that Consciousness, Itself, is the Father, the maintaining and sustaining principle of all that is.

"If so be that the Spirit of God dwell"[1] in us, then are we children of God, then are we one with the Father. The whole import of the message of The Infinite Way is to lift the individual to a state of spiritual apprehension wherein and whereby that ancient unity of oneness with the Father-consciousness is re-established. It is only the son of God, the spiritual image and likeness, who is held in the bosom of the Father. In order to achieve that relationship, we have to make that return journey of the prodigal son. We have to get up from the banquet with the swine, leave behind all those thoughts and people and doings of that swinish world, and return to the Father, abandoning mother, father, sister, and brother "for my sake." We have to abandon all our previous conceptions of life—not only our previous

[1] Romans 8:9.

concepts of sin, but our previous concepts of what constitutes good.

When you correctly understand the inner significance of the story of the prodigal son, you will have the secret of life. In the beginning, you are the Father-consciousness. You are not just a favored son in the beginning; you are one with the Father, the Father-consciousness. But you have cut yourself off to make of yourself a son separate and apart from the Father—not a son in the spiritual sense of sonship which is that of an emanation or offspring of God-consciousness, an individualization of God-consciousness, but the kind of a son who is a separate entity, who has forgotten that God is not only the Father, but God is also the son. The son in his oneness with the Father is the Father-consciousness, the all-embracing, all-embodying one infinite Consciousness.

The son has no less than all, nor is there a dividing of his inheritance with his brothers because there is no division in God. In the spiritual sense of life, the son cannot divide his inheritance any more than I can divide my understanding with you. No matter how much knowledge or understanding I impart to you, there is no diminution of that understanding or knowledge. As a matter of fact, every teacher, regardless of his field of knowledge, will tell you that the more he teaches, the more he knows. Many times, in teaching some particular aspect of his subject, a teacher finds that ideas which heretofore were not entirely clear to him are being clarified through the activity of teaching. The very act of imparting knowledge increases his own understanding.

And so we go back to our prodigal. The belief of dividing an inheritance was enough to separate him from the kingdom. In the beginning, this son who later became the prodigal was originally the Father-consciousness, but he stepped down from this high consciousness into the belief of being a son with only a part of God's allness, a divided part. With that as a beginning, it was natural that he should end up with nothing. If spending or giving is a matter of division, whatever he spent would leave him with less and less, culminating ultimately in the banquet of the husks. To return to the Father's house means to return to the consciousness of having and being one with the Father—of being that Father-consciousness. It does not mean a separate son coming back to a separate Father and receiving from a higher source: It means coming back into the realization of Father-consciousness. It means coming back into the Fatherhood-degree of consciousness, the Allness-degree.

We expand our concept of allness as we share with each other and thereby increase that which we have. We begin leaving our prodigal humanhood and come back into some measure of realization of our spiritual sonship as soon as we take our first steps in our journey along the spiritual path. As we progress along the Way, we eventually reach the Father's house which is the Father-consciousness or the consciousness of our Fatherhood. God is the consciousness of our individual being, and every one of us is in full and complete possession of the whole consciousness. Even when we share with each other, we increase that which we have.

When you realize that for yourself, you are also realizing that universally for every individual because there is only one Self. Then when people present you with pictures of incompleteness—physical, mental, moral, or financial—you enter that inner sanctuary of your own being and realize that they likewise are one with that same Father just as you are. The Father-consciousness is a universal state of being, and the awareness of this Consciousness as the maintaining and sustaining Principle of the universe is vital to the healing work.

For example, when someone calls upon you for help to secure employment, your reaction should be that no one needs employment. Why? Because God is the only one; there is no other one. God is the only Selfhood; God needs no employment. God is Self-complete, and therefore all activity must unfold from within. God, individual consciousness, embodies within Itself the fulness of the Godhead bodily. It cannot need employment; It cannot have a need of any kind except the need of realizing Its own nature. In this understanding, you will not try to do some "mental work" to secure employment for someone or to restore health to a sick body. You will abide in the center of your being in the full and complete realization of the true identity of the individual who is appearing to you as a human being.

The Son of God Is the Word Made Flesh

It is only in the sense of separateness that we fear for ourselves or for others. If I believe that God constitutes your being, can I ever fear for your being? If I fear for your being, is it not because I do not believe that you are one with the Father? Is it not because I have forgotten that you are the Word made flesh? If I fear for myself, is it not because I have accepted the belief that I am something less than God-created, God-maintained, and God-sustained? There is no disgrace in coming to these moments of fear and doubt, but every time we are touched with a doubt or fear, let us acknowledge that it could only come to us in our sense of separation from God. Therein lies the cause of the whole insecurity of the world.

But when you accept the fact that God constitutes individual being, Self-complete, Self-maintained, Self-sustained, can fear enter into your consciousness for yourself or for those who may come to you for help? Could you ever feel that you did not have enough understanding? If you know that you are the word of God made flesh and that I am the word of God made flesh, what other understanding can you need? We are Self-created, Self-maintained, Self-sustained in our infinite individuality, and fear cannot enter our thought for ourselves or for one another. Realize that God constitutes individual being; you are the Word made flesh; your patient is the Word made flesh—Self-maintained and Self-sustained.

Realize this for every individual identity—human, animal, vegetable, or mineral. If you are in the practice and are fearful for your patient, it is because you have accepted a power apart from the One, a law apart from the One, and for that matter an individual apart from the One. If, however, you are resolute in your faith and understanding that *I* am the Word made flesh, and that there is only this one *I*, universally and eternally made manifest as individual being, then you will not fear. Then when someone comes to you as a patient or a student, he is neither a patient nor a student: He is the Word made flesh, the beloved of the Father, one with the Father. You have no personal responsibility for him. You have only the responsibility of realizing in your consciousness:

> * I have no fears for you. I behold only the Father appearing as all life—the Word made flesh. In the beginning, was the Word, divine Consciousness, and all that is emanates and flows from that one infinite divine Father-consciousness. There is no power in any form of creation: The power always remains in the consciousness that formed it.
>
> God constitutes individual being—my being and your being. Need I fear for you, for me, or for anyone? Is there any power in heaven or on earth or in hell that can injure or harm the beloved son of God?
>
> No, I am one with the Father; I am the Word made flesh: My body is the Word made flesh; my business is the Word made flesh; my spiritual activity is the Word made flesh; my bank account is the Word made flesh; my friendships are the Word made flesh. Everything that concerns me is the Word made flesh; and that Word which made it flesh maintains and sustains it, and I have no personal responsibility.

If you take that attitude, then when your patient comes to you with tales of sin, disease, death, lack, limitation, wars, or rumors of wars, quickly will come the recognition, "Ah, here is only the temple of the living God. This person is the Word made flesh."

Out of the infinite divine Consciousness which you are, or which your patient is, are formed your body, your world, your sun, moon, and stars, your time and tides, your opportunities, and your fruitage. All this is formed out of the consciousness which you are. Return now from prodigality, from the belief of a separate selfhood wasting his substance; return this very minute to the realization that God constitutes your being, and that being is a Self-created, Self-maintained, and Self-sustained individuality throughout all time, all eternity, all infinity. Then you will hear a voice in your ear, "Son, thou art ever with me, and all that I have is thine."[1]

* * *

CONSCIOUSNESS UNFOLDING

A review by Henry Thomas Hamblin[2]

This is a substantial book of nearly 300 pages. Let it be said at once that this is no book for beginners, but should prove to be strong meat for those who are strong enough to accept it, and advanced enough to understand it.

Briefly, as its title implies, it deals with the unfoldment of our spiritual consciousness. Chapter 2 is devoted to peace. This will be familiar ground for our readers and students, for we have advocated over

[1] Luke 15:31.

[2] Reprinted from *The Science of Thought Review*, Bosham House, Chichester, England, March, 1958.

many years that what is needed are not metaphysical treatments or mental argument, but simply to know God's inward peace. People write asking for some magic formula which they can use in order to cure disease, unemployment, or some other form of disharmony; and some of them, I expect, are disappointed when they are told that they must relax, let go, become perfectly still and find God's inward peace and that it may flow through them like a river. They may expect some wonderful "treatment" or wordy argument; instead of which I simply "pray that they may know God's inward peace (the same peace which God Himself enjoys) and that they may be carried along on the river of God's peace, and also find God's peace flowing through them like a river." I know. of course, that nothing else is required, only to know and feel God's peace, for when this is achieved they realize that they have found God, and their own aura has become merged in the aura of God.

Whenever Joel calls to see me, the first thing he asks for is that we should have a meditation together. Not a word is spoken by either of us; we simply become quiet and enter into God's peace, the while God's peace flows through us like a river. I do not let it last for long, but Joel always says that he feels refreshed. This is not anything that *we* do, of course, it is simply the peace of God coming down and enveloping us.

It is many years since the enlightenment came to me that to "treat" for certain results, or to pray for things, was unnecessary and a waste of time and energy; and that instead, all that was needed was to find God's inward peace. Previously, I had wrestled with evil hour after hour and whole nights at a time. But at last I noticed that it was only when I entered into God's peace that the load was lifted. Then I realized that I had not to wrestle with the angel all night as Jacob did at Peniel, but only to realize God's peace. Instead of a wrestler with angels or problems, I became a spectator. I was able to stand still and see the salvation of the Lord.

It was therefore with much pleasure that I read the following in Joel's book, page 49. He is supposing that someone has come to the reader with a problem.

> Suppose that someone has come to us today with a problem. . . .
>
> Do not try to improve a person, or his health. Do not accept into your consciousness the thought that there is a person in ill health. Sit in a state of receptivity, relaxed, in a state of silence, a state of peace. Let that peace permeate your whole being, and when you have accomplished that, sit with a listening attitude, and watch the light dispel the darkness, watch intelligence dispel ignorance. Instead of your being the healer, you are a witness watching this state of peace do the healing. Be a beholder of the activity of the Christ, or God. Watch It work in us, and through us.

Still speaking about peace, Joel says, on page 60:

> Every one of you, some time or other, is going to be called upon to help somebody. Some of you are going to be called upon to help many,

and no lesson will be of greater value to you than what I am telling you now. Beginning today, at this very moment, remember: It is your consciousness that does the work for your family, for your business, for your home, for your body. It is not some far-off God. It is your own individual consciousness when your consciousness is imbued with silence and with peace. All you have to do, and all you will ever be called upon to do, is to achieve that sense of peace.

Do not wonder what great truth you ought to know. There are probably no greater truths in the world than those you already know; but there is one thing that you must practice and achieve, and that is a state of peace within your own consciousness, coupled with the realization that it is your own consciousness which is the healing Christ. When we know that *we* have the mind 'that was in Christ Jesus', then we know that we *already* have that mind which is the healing Christ; we already have that state of peace which comes from the realization that error is not power—error is not a thing. In fact, *error isn't.* You do not have to fight it, or wrestle with it, or attempt to manacle it, or sit up all night to be sure that it does not overcome you. What you must do is to learn how to find your peace.

Readers must not think because this is a big book dealing with a very deep subject that it is "hard going" or difficult reading. In fact it is far from being that, for it is most entertaining reading, and whereever one opens it one's interest is captured at once.

The author has been blest with that most rare gift of clarity combined with simplicity of expression. We shall help the sale and circulation of this book by stocking it in our book department.

* * *

TRAVELOGUE

Since our arrival in England, we have had a series of lectures and a closed class in London, with a fine group of students, many of them truly dedicated. In Manchester in the north of England, there have been more lectures and another closed class. Both our first and final lectures there had standing room only, and the class itself was a grand experience with fifty students of a very serious type, earnest in their study and practice of the message. Several students came up from London for this work. All the members of the class had been working faithfully for a long, long time and brought to the class such a depth of consciousness that this Manchester class proved to be something out of the ordinary.

A half dozen of my Masonic brothers from the English lodge in Leeds, of which I am an associate member, were in Manchester while we were there. The following week I spent an evening with the lodge in Leeds during which time Degree-work was conducted. This is the only known lodge authorized to teach esoteric Masonry, which is somewhat similar to our work of spiritually interpreting the Scriptures. To understand esoteric Masonry is to know the principles behind Masonic teachings just as the spiritual interpretation of Scripture reveals the principles of spiritual living.

The Infinite Way work is spreading so rapidly throughout the world that wherever a closed class is held there are often many in the class so new to the work that it is not always possible to attain the same fruitage as when the message is presented to students who are well-grounded in The Infinite Way. This leads me to believe that our work in the future may have to be divided so that there will be a class for those who have never before been through class and also a class for those who not only have been through classes, but who have been very earnest in their study and in their devotion to this message of The Infinite Way. In this way, I feel that the deeper teaching of The Infinite Way can more readily be given to those prepared to receive it.

Wherever we travel, I learn from students of the many different ways in which Infinite Way work began in various places—in countries, cities, and villages, here, there, and everywhere. Very often a traveler brings either a pamphlet, a book, a monthly *Letter*, or some other Infinite Way message into a community and, in this way, plants the seed out of which the activity in that particular community springs. Nearly always it is the traveler who is the pioneer and the planter of seeds.

Some of you may not know that the Hawaiian Islands were at one time volcanoes beneath the sea, raised from the bottom of the ocean to form the land which in time became the Hawaiian Islands. Originally no vegetation grew in these islands, formed of coral reef and lava rock—no trees, no flowers, no fruits. Probably coconuts floating on the surface of the ocean drifted to the Hawaiian Islands from the

South Seas and wind-borne seeds carried from great distances started the first green growth. When the Polynesians came from Samoa, centuries ago, they most likely brought fruits and flowers from the islands farther south. Again it was the traveler who planted the seeds. Then came the sailing ships from England, from Australia, from New Zealand, and later from the Philippines, China, Japan, and, of course, from North America. Each traveler brought with him his gift of some species of flowers, nuts, fruit, or other food. Each traveler planted his particular seed.

Wherever there is fertile soil, the seed takes root, whether it be the seed of a plant or the seed of an idea. Jesus planted the seed of the Word in the Holy Land, and Paul carried it to Asia Minor and southern Europe. Other disciples carried it in one direction or another. Each of these pioneers planted seeds of truth wherever he went and so carried on the great tradition which has made of the traveler a pioneer and a planter of seeds throughout the earth. And for those who remain at home, there is always work to be done to nurture, to tend, and to care for the seeds thus planted and to see that these seeds spring up into strong and powerful plants. Each fulfills his mission as it is given him to do.

As always during our visits to England, one day was spent with the Henry Thomas Hamblins, and you know the joy that we always have on such a day. The seeds Mr. Hamblin sows are planted through his books and magazine which travel throughout Europe, Asia, Africa, Australia, and New Zealand, and, of course, to Canada and the United States.

When you read this *Letter* in August, we shall be on the European continent with our students in Holland, Germany, Sweden, and perhaps Switzerland. Then after three weeks at home in September, we shall return to the mainland in October for classes in Seattle and lectures and classes in New York in November.

CHAPTER NINE: SEPTEMBER

PRAYING ARIGHT

THE importance of meditation or prayer is beginning to be recognized by men and women all over the world. Rightly understood, prayer is the most practical way of life there is; but we must not expect prayer to bring *things* to us, we must not expect to gain something *from* prayer or *through* prayer—not even happiness, joy, peace, or any of those other things that the world is seeking.

There is only one legitimate object of prayer and that is to attain God—to come face to face with God. In His presence there is fullness of life. Unless we are praying for His presence, we are not praying for fullness of life: We are praying only for little bits of life—little corners of it, trifles—but when we pray for the presence of God to fill us, to permeate us, to be ever with us, we are then praying for fulfillment in all our ways. The first essential of meditation or prayer is to know why we meditate and what to pray for. God Itself must be the goal and aim of our life, attaining which, the Master says that all things will be added unto us.

> And seek not ye what ye shall eat, or what ye shall drink, neither be ye of doubtful mind.
>
> For all these things do the nations of the world seek after: and your Father knoweth that ye have need of these things.

But rather seek ye the kingdom of God; and all these things shall be added unto you.

Fear not little flock; for it is your Father's good pleasure to give you the kingdom.

Luke 12:29-32

How can the Father know our needs except He be an infinite intelligence: How can it be His good pleasure to give us not only our needs but the whole kingdom unless He is a divine all-encompassing love. When we know God as love and intelligence, never again can we pray to God for anything; never again will we attempt to acquaint God with something that we believe we need; never can we even hope that God will do this, that, or the other thing.

The word God is not easy to understand because, although it is a short word, nevertheless, it seems to take an eternity to understand. Yet the importance of knowing God is made clear because Scripture tells us that to know Him aright is life eternal. Looking up definitions of God or reading books about Him will not teach us to know God. These are only steps leading to the experience, and when we have had that experience, then in some measure we know God and we benefit from that knowledge.

A knowledge of God leads to an entirely new concept of prayer that forever destroys the old sense of prayer which is predicated upon a withholding God, not wise enough to provide for his universe. A correct understanding of God would change our entire attitude toward life. There is nothing to tell the infinite Intelligence; there is nothing to ask the divine Love whose pleasure it is to give us the kingdom. Never again would we ask, seek, or knock for anything; but morning, noon, and night we would ask, seek, and knock for God's grace, for God's understanding, for God-awareness, for a God-experience. In other words, our entire effort would be to open ourselves to the Omnipresence which God is—the Omnipotence and Omniscience. Knowing the nature of God reveals the nature of true prayer. We shall not stop praying, but our prayers will take another form: We will eliminate all appeals from our prayers; we will eliminate all attempts to tell God, beseech God, beg, ask, or influence God. Now there is no attempt to reach God for anything.

Prayer Is Silent Receptivity

The first reaction to this new mode of prayer is that of being lost: "Now where am I? If I am not to tell God anything, what am I to do? How am I to pray?" And we shall soon learn that true prayer is not talking *to* God, but *listening* to God, *hearing* God. That reverses the entire process of prayer: No longer do we try to reach God through thought or through words; no longer do we send out a single thought or a single word in God's direction. Our attitude is wholly one of " 'Speak, Lord; for thy servant heareth.'[1] Reveal Thyself," and thus we develop within ourselves a degree of receptivity, that listening attitude which is prayer. It is not very long before the flow from within begins. Even though it

[1] I Samuel 3:9.

may not at first come in words or in visions, it will come as a feeling, a feeling that we have made the contact; or it may come as a feeling that God has made contact with us, a feeling that God has reached through into us, an awareness of God's presence and power.

It is a good idea to ponder something intangible for meditation, something that does not define itself to us. By that criterion, the Christ is an excellent subject for such a purpose because no one can describe It adequately. We may take the term "the Christ" and in a very soft, a very gentle and peaceful way, ponder it: "The Christ—the Christ—the Son of God in me—the Son of God in me is really I." Or we may ponder the word *I* until we begin to feel a softness and gentleness.

So it is that the word God is also a good word to use in meditation. No one can define what the word God means; no one can analyze it; no one can provide a chart; no one can give us a dictionary meaning that will make clear to us what God is. No one knows what God is. We can never know God with the mind, but in our innermost being, we can discern the nature of God and the function of God, and that is quite a different thing. Any contemplation or pondering of the nature of God would be a prayer, that is, it would be the first step in prayer. Quietly dwell on some of the great passages of Scripture which help to reveal the nature of God:

> He shall feed his flock like a shepherd: he shall gather the lambs with his arm, and carry them in

his bosom, and shall gently lead those that are with young.

Isaiah 40:11

God is love.

I John 4:8

. . . thy gentleness hath made me great.

Psalm 18:35

Take no thought for your life, what ye shall eat; neither for the body, what ye shall put on.

Consider the lilies how they grow: they toil not, they spin not; and yet I say unto you, that Solomon in all his glory was not arrayed like one of these.

If then God so clothe the grass, which is to day in the field, and tomorrow is cast into the oven; how much more will he clothe you, O ye of little faith?

. . . your Father knoweth that ye have need of these things.

Luke 12:22, 27, 28, 30

Whatever question is in our thought, God already knows the answer. The divine Wisdom of this universe knows all needs. The divine Love of this universe supplies all needs, and we can become aware of whatever answer or message is necessary.

Pondering such scriptural passages is a contemplation of God and the things of God; it is prayer, but it is only the first step in prayer. When we have continued in this prayerful state, keeping the mind stayed on God, then wisdom says, "Stop now, and give God a chance to break in." That is the time for the mind to become still and silent, waiting for God to speak—to sit quietly until a sense of peace descends upon us, until the inner release is felt, that deep breath, or the message for which we are waiting. Whatever form it may take, we shall know when we have received it and then we can go about our business. We have prayed—that is prayer.

Gradually, as each day comes along, we fall into the habit of trusting God's wisdom and direction: "Thank You, Father, I am not asking for anything today. I'm not telling You anything. I have no advice to give You." It is as if we were saying, "God, I'm leaving You strictly on Your own today because I really do believe that You can manage this universe without my help." Persistence in this practice leads to that moment of transition when, after we have made of ourselves a vacuum, we feel God flowing into us. We have created a vacuum which makes that possible—a vacuum of desires, a vacuum of directions to God, and a vacuum of hopes and ambitions and fears, all of which the ever flowing grace of God fills with Its peace.

We must know the principles with which we are dealing and bring them to conscious remembrance as often as possible so that in their good time they become the spirit of truth, the consciousness of truth. If we accept these principles even intellectually and are willing to struggle with them for awhile, we shall come into a spiritual awareness of them and be able to demonstrate and in a measure live them. They can only be demonstrated by you and by me individually as we make them so much a part of ourselves through prayer and meditation that they become the Comforter, and spirit of Truth, the very Christ Itself.

And what is the Christ but this very thing that happens to us after we have learned these principles and demonstrated them? It is the life that we begin to lead when we no longer have human desires or human fears, when we have no selfhood that needs glorifying, no selfhood that seeks to find a measure of adequacy by aggressively pushing itself forward, no selfhood that is constantly on the defensive because of a deep-seated feeling of inferiority. Within us will be a conscious awareness of our true identity and of our heritage as the beloved son of God. Everything that we know secretly and silently within ourselves is revealed outwardly to the world. Whatever it is that we entertain in secret, God rewards openly.

As we set aside daily periods of "listening," our affairs gradually begin to improve. The improvement may not be immediately noticeable, but as we look back a year or two later, we are struck by the changes, sometimes of a drastic nature, which have taken place in our experience: "How could all that have happened to me this year without my even being aware of it?"

A Life of Inner Communion Requires Obedience to the Laws of Spiritual Living

Many people believe that grace will come to them if only they sit around long enough waiting and hoping for it; but God's grace is functioning continuously—twenty-four hours of the day, and if we are not experiencing it, it is not because God is withholding His grace from us: It is because we are withholding ourselves from it. If we study the Bible, one good reason will be found plainly stated in the first Gospel:

> Therefore if thou bring thy gift to the altar, and there rememberest that thy brother hath ought against thee;
>
> Leave there thy gift before the altar, and go thy way; first be reconciled to thy brother, and then come and offer thy gift.
>
> Matthew 5:23, 24

God is not withholding His grace from us, but if we are not at peace with our brother, we have erected a barrier beyond which that grace cannot penetrate. We are holding somebody or something in condemnation, and if it is not a person, it is a race, a nation, or a religion. God's grace has not ceased functioning: It is we who are not permitting it to function because there is no room for God's grace in a consciousness already filled with condemnation.

As long as we are willing to see punishment inflicted on someone for his wrongs, as long as we feel that it is right for anyone to be punished, as long as we hold anyone in criticism or condemnation for his wrongdoing, just so long are we violating the laws of spiritual living taught by the Master:

> Neither do I condemn thee.
>
> John 8:11

Then came Peter to him, and said, Lord, how oft shall my brother sin against me, and I forgive him? till seven times?

Jesus saith unto him, I say not unto thee, Until seven times: but, Until seventy times seven.

Matthew 18:21, 22

Be ye therefore merciful, as your Father also is merciful.

Judge not, and ye shall not be judged: condemn not, and ye shall not be condemned: forgive, and ye shall be forgiven.

Luke 6:36, 37

In the entire New Testament, there is no record of the Master's ever saying to a sick person, "Your sins have done this to you, or your wrong thinking has done this to you, or not going to church has done this to you, or belonging to the wrong church, or meeting people who belong to the wrong church." No, none of these things can be found in the Gospels. In the four Gospels, we learn that God's blessing falls upon sinner as well as saint: "He maketh his sun to rise on the evil and on the good, and sendeth rain on the just and on the unjust."[1] God is functioning as a continuous state of being. If we are not enjoying the grace of God, it has nothing to do with God; it is we who have removed ourselves from that grace.

In proportion as we make an effort to purge ourselves of self—self-seeking, criticism, and condemnation—in that proportion does our inner communion bear fruit. Furthermore, the more we commune

[1] Matthew 5:45.

inwardly, the more are we purged of negative traits of character, of our human emotions and feelings.

The inner communion helps to purify us, but a little conscious effort toward controlling our grosser feelings also helps us to reach that deeper communion.

Inner communion results in an outer activity of harmony and peace, but no one can live in that inner communion if he is violating such spiritual laws as those that have been revealed by Christ Jesus. No one can expect to live an inner life of communion with signs following if, at the same time, he is hating his fellow-man, entertaining prejudice or bigotry, indulging in miserliness, or withholding forgiveness, understanding, or cooperation. Inner communion under such circumstances is an impossibility.

Establishing a Conscious Awareness of the Presence

In the early morning hours, before the day's activities have begun, we must be sure that we have established ourselves in God's grace and that we are in the rhythm of God-consciousness. Therefore, in order to do this we find a quiet place and begin our day with prayer. Perhaps the first thing that comes to thought is:

> * God is closer to me than breathing, nearer than hands and feet, so I do not have to bring God to me and I do not have to go anywhere to be in the presence of God. Here where I am, God is. This will be true all the day long, wherever I am. Here

where I am, there where I am, anywhere I am, God is, always closer than breathing, Omnipresence Itself. "The angel of the Lord encampeth round about"[1] me. My trust, my confidence, and my hope are in Him who is round about me "as the mountains are round about Jerusalem."[2] So I know now that God's grace is with me, wherever I am.

Of what does that grace consist? It is a power, a presence—the presence of all-good. God is power—all power, the only power. Nothing, not even drunken drivers on the road, can have power; not even falling bombs can have power: Only God has power—only God. Not even my mistakes have power: Only God has power. I have all the power of God with me in every activity, in every experience, in every transaction, in every journey. Every step of my way, I have Omnipresence—Omnipotence. I have the all-knowing Intelligence and the divine Love that is willing and waiting to give me the kindgom.

The first half of our prayer is this conscious recognition of the presence of God, but the second half is when we sit quietly, gently feeling an all-embracing peace descend upon us, and we hear, "Every word you said is true! *I* will never leave you nor forsake you." Then we can go about our day's work: We have prayed—we have prayed ourselves into the very kingdom of heaven; we have prayed ourselves into God's grace.

It may be necessary at noon or in the afternoon or

[1] Psalm 34:7. [2] Psalm 125:2.

evening when the distresses of the day crowd in to re-establish this contact. Again we turn within. This time something of a quite different nature may come: "What have I against any man, and what has any man against me?" Immediately we begin inwardly to make peace:

> * God is love. God is forever loving; God's love is flowing through me to all this world. God's forgiveness touches everyone—the man born blind, the thief on the cross, the woman taken in adultery, the leper. God's grace is a state of forgiveness for everybody, and God's love and God's forgiveness flow through me to all the world.

In this meditation, we have made peace with our brother, and now our prayer is fruitful. Again, that is only the first half of the prayer: The second half is sitting in the silence, receptive, responsive, waiting until the flow begins. Suddenly we are lifted up and we know that we are in the kingdom of God; nothing can come nigh our dwelling place to injure or to harm. Our whole prayer is one of inner communion. Not once have we asked God for anything; not once have we told God anything; not once have we tried to influence God.

Soon we shall find that we cannot stay away from prayer for very long. We shall be praying three times, four, five, ten times every day. Ultimately we shall not even be able to sleep through the night because the desire for that inner communion will be so strong that we will awaken two or three times during the night to renew and enjoy it. Prayer becomes a continuing activity of consciousness. This is what Paul meant when he said, "Pray without ceasing"[1]—live always in prayer, always in communion with the Father. We shall never know what the Father wants for us unless we are living in an inner communion, waiting for an unfoldment.

Fruits of Prayer

Truth attracts unto itself. There is an invisible bond drawing to each his own. The secret of that is conscious oneness with God. If within ourselves in meditation we achieve an inner communion with God, we are then in touch with everyone in the world whom we can bless or who can bless us. We do not have to know anyone, and no one has to know us; but if we sit in our inner sanctuary with the door closed and there commune with the Father within, we shall find when we open our door that "the multitudes" have come seeking whatever it is that we have.

That is the revelation of the Sermon on the Mount. We do not have to use human modes or means; we do not have to ask one another for anything: All we have to do is to live in an inner communion and obey the impulses welling up from within. We do not have to tell man, whose breath is in his nostrils what we have need of, because man whose breath is in his nostrils does not want to and would not give it to us anyway. The Spirit of God realized in consciousness has a way of searching out just the right place, the right person, the right way, or the right activity and of bringing it into our experience. Let us live in

[1] I Thessalonians 5:17.

that inner communion and let our needs be filled from within.

To know how much God can do for those who rightly pray, it is only necessary to meet some of the mystics of the world and see the joy that is theirs, witness the inner peace—the happiness and the glory, and above all, see the love that exists among them, whether they are white, black, or yellow, whether they are Jew or Christian, Mohammedan or Hindu. For them, there are no such divisions. In communing with God, they have communed with their fellow-man and they find that their fellow-man has neither race, religion, class, creed, nor other distinction. In Spirit, all are united in oneness.

When a person establishes any kind of contact or relationship with God, he immediately comes into a complete, perfect, and harmonious relationship with others. In my own experience, I have found that in proportion as I attained a conscious realization of God's presence, a conscious oneness or unity with God, I likewise attained a oneness with man—with all men, women, and children—with animals, and in fact, even with the mineral kingdom. Everyone and everything responded. Conscious oneness with God constitutes oneness with all spiritual being. As we attain some measure of conscious oneness with our Source, we attain the divine grace that naturally follows such an experience and we find our Self-completeness in God.

It is true, however, that this experience of conscious oneness with God and eventually conscious union with God comes only in proportion to our individual devotion to that task—through a great devotion to God, to meditation, and to service to our fellow-man. In other words, we cannot study and hope to demonstrate this principle and yet not live it. There is no way to use these beautiful words in a prayer while our lives are bearing opposite testimony to the words we speak. Nothing gives such satisfaction, such joy, such pleasure, such peace, such health, and such an abundance of supply as attaining at least some measure of conscious union with our Source, with that which we call God.

Those who live and move and have their being in God-consciousness, those who pray without ceasing are the people who find that the Spirit of the Lord descends upon them, and through this Spirit of God they are able to heal: They are able to comfort the mourner; they are able to supply the hungry; they are able to bring joy to the sorrowing. And upon whom shall the Spirit of the Lord descend except those who open their consciousness to the inflow of that divine Spirit?

"Where the Spirit of the Lord is, there is liberty"[1] —no bondage of any kind: no bondage to poverty, no bondage to war, no bondage to sin, no bondage to disease. Wherever God is entertained in consciousness, there is where the Spirit of the Lord is. But when we permit hour after hour of the day to pass without a conscious acknowledgment of God's presence and power, without recognizing God as the source of our life, the source of our food, the source of our health, harmony, and being, we are

[1] II Corinthians 3:17.

living as though we were completely cut off from God.

The goal of The Infinite Way is attaining that conscious realization of God's presence—the Spirit of the Lord. As that Spirit of the Lord descends upon us, it works through our mind and heart and soul and being and body to bless all those with whom we come in contact, that is, all those who have any receptivity at all to the spiritual way of life.

Open your consciousness to the inflow of the divine Spirit which is already within you, which is awaiting your own recognition and acknowledgment. Then be patient for a few weeks or months until that Spirit begins to flow out in a continuous stream, and you will find that if your business has been broken, it will be raised up again; if your home has been broken, it will be raised up again; if your health has been broken, it will be raised up again; if age has descended upon you, it will flee, and youth return. All this happens as the Spirit of God descends upon you.

Go within, become quiet and still until the peace that passeth understanding fills your heart and mind and soul. Wherever the Spirit of the Lord is, there is holy ground, and all those who come within the range of a consciousness imbued with It, feel It. In the presence of that Spirit, there is liberty: There is freedom from all limitation, freedom from all discords, freedom from all inharmony.

A review of *Practicing the Presence*[1]

Alfred C. Ames

Practicing the Presence is addressed to those religious seekers who are receptive to mysticism. Here are asserted the reality of God, the divinity within each human being, the identity of spirit among men and between them and God. Any dubious reader is invited to be still and wait upon the stirrings of his own spirit.

Joel Goldsmith writes with the confidence of experience and the awareness that a long series of mystical writers have proclaimed substantially the same message. His style is simple, colloquial, spontaneous, and serious. It is not studied and finds its figures of speech more often in biblical than in original phrasing. The over-all effect is one of clarity and directness and close relationship to the Christian scriptures.

The book will not be congenial to irreligious readers, or to all varieties of religious experience. But those prepared to accept the idea of an immanent God will find light and leading here for the further development of mystical insight. For congenial readers, Goldsmith can appear a major prophet with power to make the crooked straight and the rough places plain.

[1] Reprinted from *The Magazine of Books, Chicago Sunday Tribune*, June 22, 1958.

It is now July 11, and here we are in Kyles of Lochalsh, Ross-shire, Scotland, where Emma and I are enjoying two delightful weeks of vacation, driving throughout most of Scotland with two students who have been a part of The Infinite Way work since my first trip here. We are "doing" the lakes and glens, the mountains and valleys, drinking in the beauty in its many forms and varieties. Scotland is an ideal vacation land. Among its many attractions are the quiet, the absence of heavy travel, and the clean, brisk air. Even the present "heat wave" has not gone above the middle 60's.

The London and Manchester work was so well attended that, on July 18, we are returning to London where I shall give another series of student-talks and another closed class beginning July 26. Then we go on to the Continent—Holland, Germany, and Switzerland—returning home September 1, for three weeks, after which we leave for Seattle, Washington; Victoria and Vancouver, British Columbia; New York City; and back to Hawaii again for the holidays. Forty-two weeks of travel out of the fifty-two in 1958—and only you can measure its worth!

Today, in meditation, the picture of this entire travel-year flashed before me and with it the question, "Why?" Instantly came the answer: To bring "*My* kingdom" to the conscious awareness of those who will hear, to reveal Omnipresence, the realm of Soul, the Kingdom where peace, joy, and harmony are the realized experience of those who enter. I "saw" so clearly that The Infinite Way is telling once more of that Kingdom which each one may discover at the center of his being and of the steps necessary to the unveiling of this spiritual consciousness. "This world" has defeated itself by attempting to acquire or attain this Kingdom, but it cannot be acquired or attained: It must be released from within.

In my travels, I find myself repeating the Master's teaching of the nature of God and of our true identity: forgiving; blessing those who hate us; praying for our enemies; praying in secret; doing our alms in secret; seeking God-realization in place of material demonstration; loving our neighbor through service, whether the service be that of outer forms or of inner prayer, since each must serve at the present level of his consciousness. The Infinite Way gives us the secret of the nature of the errors of "this world" and teaches us how to translate them into the "arm of flesh." Herein is the secret of spiritual healing and spiritual living. Without this awareness, truth is reduced to the level of just another philosophy, words without power. Without this knowledge, how will we ever learn the lesson of this *Letter*—how will we ever learn to pray aright?

By the fruits of our work, the travels will be justified: "Ye see then how that by works a man is justified, and not by faith only. . . . faith without works is dead." Are we bringing the kingdom of God —"*My* kingdom"—into tangible expression in our lives? Are we "dying daily" to the ways of "this world"? Are we receiving more spiritual grace—the life lived without taking thought? Is the deep, cool well of contentment bringing the waters of life to our experience? Are we experiencing the green pastures and still waters of "*My* Kingdom"?

CHAPTER TEN: OCTOBER

BREAK THE FETTERS THAT BIND YOU

MANY of the difficulties and struggles in our experience come because we are living on different planes of consciousness, sometimes on one and sometimes on another, and often these planes are in conflict one with another. On one plane we are physical beings with minds, the body being the dominant factor; on another plane we are mental beings with bodies, that is, we are a mind and a body, and the body is governed by the mind. It may be governed by a conscious activity of mind or it may be by an involuntary activity of mind.

In recent months, there have been many accounts in magazines and newspapers of the experiments which have been conducted in the area of subliminal perception through the medium of television and the motion picture. In the first experiments, which were held inside a moving picture theatre, the audience was instructed to go into the lobby during the intermission to buy popcorn and coca cola. Even though they did not know such a suggestion had been given to them, because the slide had been flashed across the screen so rapidly that it was invisible to the eyes and, therefore, did not register consciously in the mind, the majority of those in the theatre were impelled to obey this suggestion. Whether or not they wanted the popcorn or coca cola made no difference. The impulsion was so strong that they felt compelled to go out and buy it, giving their good money for something they may not have wanted and otherwise would not have bought. It was not necessary for them to be aware of the suggestion, to see or to hear it, and there was no knowledge that it was even being made.

If a person is not alert, he will obey such subtly given instructions because this technique is not aimed at the conscious mind; it is aimed at the subconscious. These experiments show the extent to which the body obeys the dictates of the mind. On the human level of consciousness, that is exactly what happens. The body is subject to the mind. On this same level of consciousness, there are certain laws, mental and physical, which if violated bring punishment. This is the law of cause and effect: "Whatsoever a man soweth, that shall he also reap"[1]—as you do to others so will it be done unto you. All this is because, as human beings, we live on a mental plane, and even the body is subject to mental control.

The Mind, Ignorant of Truth, Is an Easy Prey to World-Beliefs

Every discord is the result of the violation of some law on the human plane, mental or physical. If there were no violation of law there would be no inharmony—no disease, no sin. Some kind of a law is always being violated: Sitting in a draft or getting the feet wet results in catching cold; exposure to contagion results in disease; injudicious eating

[1] Galatians 6:7.

results in functional disorders. These are mental laws which have been laid down and, just as the subject in the experiments with subliminal perception is unaware of the suggestions being thrust at him, so it is not necessary to know these mental and physical laws to be affected by them and to suffer the penalty their violation brings.

There are thousands of laws of which people may be unaware, and yet when they are violated, a penalty follows: A newborn child may know nothing of the ill effects of drafts, but if he happens to be in a draft, he is likely to catch cold. Obviously an infant would know nothing of the existence of such a law, but it is not necessary to know that there is a law or that it is being violated in order to come under its penalty.

All the error in this world is as universal and as invisible as the slides flashed upon the screen in the experiments with subliminal perception, and it operates in the same manner—without a conscious awareness of it. That makes everybody a victim of it. As a matter of fact, everybody born into this world is a victim of all the unknown laws lodged in human consciousness. Almost from the moment of conception, a person's consciousness is being filled with beliefs of power in people and conditions, and his acceptance of these beliefs makes him a victim of them.

Hawaiians know that the work of the good and bad kahunas is effective primarily because of individual fear or belief in their power. The aborigines of Australia engage in much the same practice under the name of black magic, and whereas the kahuna in Hawaii might cast his spell with a piece of fingernail or a hair, the black magician of the aborigines accomplishes the same results by pointing. He either points his finger or a sharp piece of wood in the direction of the victim, and the moment he does that, his victim becomes ill and in a few days dies. Why? Certainly not because there is any power in kahunaism and not because there is any power in black magic, but only because they have been accepted and feared as a power. Sin and disease operate in the world in the same way as kahunaism does—by suggestion. We do not have to know that the suggestion has been made; we only have to believe that the thoughts and things of the world are power.

Originally metaphysical healing rested on the principle of truth dispelling error or truth over error. The basic idea was that if evil thoughts entertained in the mind had an effect on the body, how much greater an effect would good thoughts have on the body. On that theory, a religion sprang up—the religion of right thinking. It is founded on the idea that, under ordinary circumstances, the human race is a victim of whatever beliefs are circulating in consciousness. For example, if an epidemic is rampant in one part of the world, it soon spreads throughout the world because, according to adherents of this teaching, wherever there are people to think, there are people to accept the result of thought. Metaphysicians argued that, if people throughout the world are an easy prey to erroneous suggestions, truth or right thinking should have an equally great effect upon the body, only it would be of a beneficial nature.

Out of this teaching in which the individual filled his consciousness with truth, which acted therapeutically upon the body and which was found to be very effective, grew psychosomatic medicine, founded on similar principles. It used psychological healing, that is, changing the patient's attitude from a negative to a positive base, a technique of filling consciousness with truth as against having it filled with erroneous beliefs and theories. A mind imbued with error, wrong thinking or negative thinking, produces a negative condition of body, pocketbook, or of family life; a mind imbued with truth results in a healthy body, a healthy purse, or a healthy family life. In other words, it is a question now of decision whether one is going to wake up in the morning and accept any or every thought that comes to him, or whether he is going to take a positive stand and reject the negative.

This type of practice has been a step in the right direction because it has been a movement away from leaving one's mind a blank for the world to act upon. If a person has a mind which merely accepts everything that is given to it orally, visually, or invisibly, that mind can be acted upon and made to follow the dictates of an imposed thought—of suggestion. The individual who has determined that he will do his own thinking and will be moved or governed only by what he, himself, accepts has started on a new path. The effects of world-belief become less of a dominating factor in such a person's experience. Truth-students, regardless of which truth-teaching they may follow, are less frequently victims of this universal mesmerism than is the world at large and, furthermore, they are less affected by the conditions of the world.

Refuse to Accept World-Beliefs as Power

Everyone must learn to awaken in the morning and take hold of his own mind by realizing:

> *Nothing can enter my mind from without because my mind is an instrument through which *I* function—not an instrument through which somebody else functions or through which world-belief functions. My mind is an instrument given to me just as my body is given to me, and just as I keep my body inviolate so I keep my mind inviolate, free from world-beliefs. I do not permit my mind to be used by suggestion, by outside influences, or by outside opinions or theories. I make my mind an instrument for the truth of God. My mind is an instrument through which *I* function.

This realization cannot be achieved through a blind faith that God will take care of us. It must be done consciously. If we are to be saved from these world-influences, these mesmeric influences like disease and death, it is not going to be God who is going to save us from them. It will be because we refuse to let our mind be acted upon by world-beliefs and hold our mind open only to God.

If we dwell—live, move, and have our being—in the secret place of the most High, none of the evils of the world will come nigh our dwelling place. They will not happen to us if we are living in obedience to the principle of keeping consciousness filled with truth, if we are refusing to accept world-beliefs as power and are realizing that the only power operating within us is the power of truth. Whether or not we consciously know a specific truth is not the point. The point is whether or not we know that the truth operating in our consciousness is power and that nothing else is.

Among many truth-students, there is too much superstition, far too much blind faith that there is some kind of a God who does something for metaphysical students that He does not do for other people. That is a fatal belief. God is God, and God is no respecter of persons. God is available to white or black, Jew or Christian, Mohammedan or Hindu. God is available to anyone on the face of the globe, to anyone who makes himself consciously one with Him. It has nothing to do with God. The question is whether an individual believes that he is living as a human being in a world where hypnotism—a kind of subliminal perception—has been going on for generations, going on unknown to us as individuals, yet operative in our consciousness or in what the psychologists now call the subconscious; or whether he recognizes that his mind is not subject to the suggestions and vagaries of world-beliefs, but is a transparency through which God functions.

Seventy-five to eighty years of metaphysical practice prove that ninety percent of the world's errors can be avoided in proportion as we take hold of ourselves and *consciously, consciously recognize no power but one,* and that power not external to us, operating upon us, but within us, operating outward from us. The room in which we are sitting at this very moment may be filled with all the error that exists anywhere in the world. At this very moment, it may be filled with the atmosphere of death, disease, accident, sin, and false appetite. These suggestions are not only pouring in from the radio and television, but they are pouring in through the world-consciousness. Not knowing this, we may become victims of them in one form or another, but knowing it, we can protect ourselves from their effects.

Watch what happens in your own experience when you learn to awaken in the morning and absolutely bar from yourself the possibility of world-thought entering your consciousness and operating in your experience. "Ye shall know the truth, and the truth shall make you free."[1] A thousand shall fall at your left hand and ten thousand at your right hand, but it shall not come nigh those who dwell in this truth. There have always been wars and rumors of wars; there have been plagues, droughts, floods, and storms; and yet Scripture says that none of these things shall come nigh your dwelling place. Anyone who is willing to go to the trouble of giving sufficient time every day to the recognition that even though world-beliefs exist they do not exist as power can experience a measure of this immunity promised in Scripture:

*World-beliefs can find no entrance into my consciousness because my consciousness is Truth expressing Itself. No human theories, beliefs,

[1] John 8:32.

laws, or hypnotic suggestions can enter my consciousness to defile or to make a lie. All power—the power of Good, or God—flows out from within me to this world.

Hypnotism is not truth, and if we learn to abide in spiritual truth and apply that truth to every experience of daily living, negative thoughts and things that operate in the world through universal mesmerism will be nullified. As long as our consciousness is filled with truth, we cannot be made to accept a lie. When we maintain our mind as a temple of God and let nothing enter that mind except what comes from God, we shall find that we are living in an inner peace.

Whether that human experience will be harmonious or inharmonious, whether it will be successful or unsuccessful, whether it will be good or evil is determined by us. We determine that by our willingness to set aside some part of every hour to remind ourselves that we are not victims of whatever it is that is floating around in the air, whether thoughts or things, but that we are the outlet for the presence and power of God. Our mind is the temple of God, just as is our body, and we maintain its sanctity.

Everyone on the human plane is acting and reacting to some suggestion of universal belief. Humanly, we are antennas and respond to another person's thoughts, moods, and disposition; we react to one another's feelings as well as to world-feelings and world-tensions. When other people fear something collectively or individually, we fear the same thing; but once we recognize that tendency, we become less and less responsive to outside influences. A person who does not understand that there are unseen forces governing his human experience would, of course, be unwilling to spend even five minutes of his time in an effort to become immune to world-beliefs. But once we begin to perceive that there are many things that we do that we do not really intend doing or do not want to do and that we think many thoughts that are contrary to our nature and which must have been imposed upon us from without, then we shall begin to see that there is a universal mesmerism and we shall be willing to make the effort necessary to free ourselves from it:

> *Universal mesmerism is not a power that can enter my consciousness; it seems to be a power and acts like a power only because of my ignorance of its nature. Now that I recognize it for what it is, I no longer respond to it, I no longer accept its suggestions, I no longer react to it. I am the temple of the living God, and all that the Father is flows through me.

Attaining the Higher Dimension of Life

There is another plane of consciousness which Jesus referred to as "*My* kingdom." This is the plane of consciousness in which The Infinite Way functions in your life after you have assimilated and proved in some measure the correct letter of truth as taught in our writings and recordings. Without the attainment of the knowledge of the correct letter of truth and its proof in your experience, it is almost impossible to attain the spirit of truth, the actual consciousness of truth, which is the "My kingdom' —the spiritual kingdom, or consciousness.

"My kingdom is not of this world"[1]—not of the mental and physical world. In this kingdom, there is a peace that can never be known with the mind or body: "My peace I give unto you: not as the world giveth, give I unto you."[2] This is an entirely different realm of consciousness. In this higher consciousness, there is only being: There are no laws; there is no cause and no effect; there is neither good nor evil, up nor down. There is just being. Strangely enough when "My kingdom" or "My peace" can be brought even into the mind, it nullifies human law and removes the penalties for its transgression because it removes the transgression itself. Watch the change which occurs when you make yourself consciously one with God, when you open yourself and become a state of receptivity to everything that flows from the kingdom of God within, thereby consciously shutting yourself off from the world's mesmeric influence.

The higher dimension of life to which the Master referred as "My kingdom" is not accessible to the person who is under world-mesmerism. As that mesmerism is dispelled and we become as conscious of God operating in us as heretofore we were conscious of fear, doubt, suspicion, hate, envy, jealousy, we become susceptible to the activity of the kingdom of God. Those who understand how world-mesmerism, or universal hypnotism, operates are able to nullify its effects in their experience.

It is folly for a human being whose eyes are not

[1] John 18:36. [2] John 14:27.

open and who does not perceive clearly the nature of this universal sense to think that, by going through the forms of meditation, he is going to hear the still small voice. It is folly for the person who is still indulging in personal sense—hate, envy, jealousy, malice, prejudice—to believe that he can sit down, close his eyes, and immediately God will be on the scene to protect him. This is not possible until a person has separated himself from the very influences that originally created a sense of separation from God. We are only separated from God because the mind, instead of being a clear transparency for the Soul, has become clouded by personal sense or world-mesmerism. In such a state of hypnotism, God cannot be heard.

Non-Reaction Is the Measure of Our Freedom from World-Beliefs

We can help each other over many and many a hard place, but this can only be done to the extent that we are no longer being used by personal sense, by a universal hypnotism, which fills our minds, thoughts, and even bodies with world-beliefs. It takes months before we can separate ourselves from these universal beliefs and become receptive and responsive to the still small voice within; but after a few weeks of practice, we begin to be less and less receptive and responsive to some of these world-urges. It really takes months of work, however, before we arrive at a state of consciousness which does not respond to those things which the world is fearing, which is indifferent to certain things which, heretofore, aroused anger, resentment, rebellion, or a desire for revenge, or which does not react to greed, selfishness, or sensuality.

Learn this lesson well! The human world and the people in it are victims of world-mesmerism—victims of every negative, diseased, sinful, and poverty-stricken state of thought that operates as human consciousness—and it strikes at us wherever we are weakest. If it is a fear of disease, world-mesmerism will take the form of some kind of illness; if it is a fear of lack, world-mesmerism will take the form of poverty or limitation; if it is false appetite, world-mesmerism will take the form of alcoholism, drug-addiction, or even gluttony: World-mesmerism will always find its way to our most vulnerable—our weakest—spot. If nothing else, it will make us fear a ghost somewhere.

Our work as students is to obey the Master's injunction to come out and be separate: "I pray not that thou shouldest take them out of the world, but that thou shouldest keep them from the evil. They are not of the world, even as I am not of the world."[1] When we are responding less and less to the world's impulses and the world's fears, the world's doubts, and the world's sin, lacks, and diseases; when we have more and more immunity; when we go through life less and less aware that those things are going on around us, or if we are aware of them, they make no impression upon us; then we know that we are being freed from world-mesmerism and are now in the world but not of it. We are now of the kingdom of God: Now the still small voice can take over and direct us and lead us into green pastures, beside the

[1] John 17:15, 16.

still waters; now the inner spiritual impulse can do those things for us which Scripture promises.

No one can do this for us. We alone can free ourselves of the hypnotism of this world. When we ask for help from a practitioner, the practitioner can give us help on that particular problem at that particular minute. A practitioner may nullify some form of error or break some form of hypnotism for us, however, only to make room for other forms. Why? Because we have not freed ourselves from the invisible influence that exists as universal hypnotism.

Hypnotism Is Not a Power

Do not make the mistake, however, of fearing this invisible influence, for it is not a power except to those who are either ignorant of it or to those who give it power. It is not a power once its nature is realized. At this stage of our experience, we should be able to shut ourselves out from world-hypnotism just as we can turn our radio to any station we want or turn it off completely. It may take us a few months or longer to arrive at this stage of consciousness, but it can only be accomplished if it is practiced faithfully many times a day.

When something says, "I have a headache," our immediate response must be, "No, it is not I who have a headache. This is universal sense striking at me." Or if the suggestion comes, "I have a lack that I cannot fill," the answer is, "No, it is not I who have the lack. I am accepting a universal sense of lack." We shall not only be in the world, but of it, until we break the hypnotic sense that makes us the victim of this silent thing that is going on.

For thousands of years, the human race has believed things that are not true: The world was flat; the sun revolved around the earth; wars and pestilence were necessary to decrease the population so that the population would not exceed the forseeable food supply. Then some enlightened person—someone with vision—was able to see beyond the appearance and disprove some theory which heretofore had been accepted as law—astronomical, geographic, economic, medical, or dietary.

We do not have to accept limitation in any form—limitation of health, of pocketbook, or of human relationships. We do not have to accept limitation in any form because these limitations are merely man-made beliefs which have no more foundation than the many theories which at one time were considered sound, but which today are dismissed as ludicrous. We must stand on the truth that I and the Father are one and all that the Father has is ours. We must realize our infinity and prove it. But this can only be demonstrated as we realize that we have been victimized, not by lack, but by a universal suggestion which we have ignorantly accepted.

Much of the foregoing comes under the heading of what we call protective work, but that is a misnomer because the term "protective work" implies that there is some power from which to be protected. What we need to be protected from is our ignorance of our true identity, our ignorance of the source of true wisdom. Many of the things we believe are not true at all: Many of the things we believe about each other and many of the things we believe about the world are not true at all. As one writer said almost a hundred years ago, "The trouble with people is not that they don't know, but that they know so much that ain't so." In order to know how much blasphemy and how much bearing of false witness against our neighbor there is in the world, it is only necessary to travel and meet people of the world. They are not at all what the world would have us believe they are.

We must stop accepting world-hypnotism. We must realize that we have been accepting what the world pumps into us silently and invisibly, accepting it as if it were fact, instead of turning to God and letting God reveal the truth: "Father, what is the truth about this individual or this condition?"

Usually, when we do this in humility and sincerity, the answer will come back, "This is My child, My beloved child in whom *I* am well-pleased. This is My temple."

On the whole, what we believe about each other is not true. It is what is revealed to us from within that comes with authority, and that will come only when we have sufficiently come out from among them and become separate:

> *Nothing can enter my being that defileth or maketh a lie for I and the Father are one. I am subject only unto the law and life of God, the wisdom of God, the mind of God, the Soul of God. *I* am in the midst of me, and from that *I* comes my wisdom, my direction, my guidance, my protection, my sustenance. I turn only to It and I am led and fed by It.

When Darwin first presented his theory of the origin of mankind, it received very little attention and that of a negative nature. Years later, the theory exploded in the minds of scholars, and a new era began. The few thousand words which you have just read in this *Letter* embody one of the most important principles of my lifework. These words you may receive with as much indifference as many received the result of Darwin's lifework. They may make as slight an impact upon you today as Darwin's explosive theory made upon his contemporaries a hundred years ago. But if you will read and study this message and glimpse its underlying truth, the substance of this *Letter* may prove to be a turning point in your life and may be the means of ushering in a new day in your experience. The years of my life spent in the search for truth led to the discovery of the principles of The Infinite Way, and whatever success has attended the work has been the result of the practice of these principles.

This October *Letter* is going into only about 5000 homes in all the world, but remember that in these homes there are students prepared to receive this message. The extent to which you accept and prove these principles will determine how rapidly the next 5000 homes will open themselves to the harmony available through living The Infinite Way by means of the practice of these principles.

SPECIAL ANNOUNCEMENT

While in Holland, an inner experience began which continues to unfold. I have therefore cancelled all remaining lecture and class work for 1958 and shall remain at home in Hawaii and care for my mail, healing work, and manuscripts until the next "call" comes to travel.

As the months roll around, I shall continue to tell you of the work just completed in Europe where The Infinite Way took a tremendous leap forward in depth and spread of activity.

Prepare with me by studying thoroughly the 1958 work: The Adelaide Closed Class, two Chicago and one New York Closed Classes, The London Open Class, The London Advanced Class, and The Manchester Closed Class.

Humanly speaking, I am truly sorry not to be with you this October and November as we had planned—but spiritually we must rejoice together for it is for your spiritual unfoldment, for the message of The Infinite Way, and for me that this experience has come about.

The entire European experience this year lifted me into the consciousness which culminated in Holland as the beginning of that which is now taking place.

We have October, November, and December in which to prepare for what is to be given us by divine Grace.

Both in London and in Manchester the work has outgrown the lecture and class rooms now being used, and next year will find us seeking larger facilities. This is in keeping with what we witnessed in Australia early this year. While it has not been possible to travel to South Africa during the past two years, the news from Johannesburg and Capetown is also one of expansion.

Lift up your eyes, and look on the fields; for they are white already to harvest.

John 4:35

The harvest truly is great, but the labourers are few.

Luke 10:2

Yes, even with all this expansion, the labourers are few. Let us practice faithfully the principles of The Infinite Way that we may be fit labourers in the Father's vineyard.

CHAPTER ELEVEN: NOVEMBER

THE FRUITS OF THE SPIRIT

SETTING aside a special day or days to give thanks for blessings received is not a practice limited to the United States alone. Many years before the Pilgrims came to this country, old England celebrated the gathering in of the harvest in the fall of the year. Even the ancients practiced this rite. As long as there has been recorded history, it has been the custom to observe a festival of thanksgiving in gratitude for the harvest which has been reaped.

While students of spiritual wisdom do not confine the giving of thanks to a single day of the year, but let every day be a day of thanksgiving; nevertheless, it is not inappropriate at this season to consider the kind of harvest you, as a student of the spiritual way of life, are garnering into your spiritual storehouse. This will not be measured in terms of outward good, although that may well be one evidence of spiritual fruitage. If your harvest has been scant, engage in a little soul-searching introspection to see wherein you have failed; if abundant, rejoice in the greater awareness of the Presence which has made this possible. Always evaluate your progress in terms of spiritual fruitage:

> But the fruit of the Spirit is love, joy, peace, longsuffering, gentleness, goodness, faith,

Meekness, temperance: against such there is no law.

Galatians 5:22, 23

Abide in me, and I in you. As the branch cannot bear fruit of itself, except it abide in the vine; no more can ye, except ye abide in me.

I am the vine, ye are the branches: He that abideth in me, and I in him, the same bringeth forth much fruit . . .

Herein is my Father glorified, that ye bear much fruit . . .

John 15:4, 5, 8

There is no way to taste of the fruit of the Spirit except through the word of God, the word of God which in the midst of you is mighty. If you abide in the Word and let the Word abide in you, you will bear fruit richly. But the word of God is not something that you can read in a book; the word of God is not something you may have memorized: The Word itself must come from the mouth of God. The still small voice must utter itself to you within you, and when that word of God comes to you, it comes with power and with signs following.

The Word Becomes Tangible Experience

The Word coming to human consciousness becomes flesh, and life in the outer realm begins to transform itself into the pattern of spiritual demonstration. That word of God which you have received in your consciousness becomes the flesh of your body, the substance of your pocketbook, the activity of your business, and the bond in your human relationships. It is your daily bread, the manna which falls day by day. Learn never to depend upon yesterday's manna. Learn to go to God and pray:

> *"Give us this day our daily bread"[1]—give us this day the staff of life, the word of God, vital and alive, the spiritual Word, the spiritual Presence, the spiritual Power. Every day, Lord, give us of Thy word; let us drink of the fountain of life; let us eat of this inner meat that the world knows not of—the substance of life which is the word of God. "Man shall not live by bread alone, but by every word of God."[2]

The Word, then, is the bread; the Word is the substance; the Word is the wine; the Word is the blood; the Word is the meat; the Word is the water. Pray for the Spirit, for the Word. The fruits of that Spirit come to you, first of all, in the form of the word of God entering your consciousness. This may be an audible word; it may be an impression or a feeling; it may be a release; it may be a deep breath. Regardless of how it comes, you will recognize that it is the presence of God which you have experienced.

Therefore, when you pray, pray only for the Word, and the fruits of that spiritual Word will be peace, joy, health, harmony, wholeness, abundance, and infinite good. Pray only for the Spirit; pray that the Spirit of God dwell in you that you may be the child of God, and if the child of God, heir, and if heir, joint-heir to all the heavenly riches. Pray that the

[1] Matthew 6:11. [2] Luke 4:4.

Spirit of the Lord be upon you so that you may be ordained to heal the sick and comfort the mourner. Pray that His grace be realized as your sufficiency. This is spiritual prayer, and the fruitage of it is joy, peace, harmony, abundance, wholeness, completeness, perfection, and oneness.

God is glorified in the fruitage of our lives, and in no other way is God glorified. In proportion as we live in this Word and let it live in us, do we experience a harmonious, fruitful, human life. True, there may be problems, but what of it? No one is promised complete immunity from the discords of life while he is on earth living a human life. Problems must inevitably arise, but they can only be a blessing because it is through these problems that we rise higher in consciousness, and through that rising, harmony is brought into our daily life.

The experiences that come to us when we live in obedience to the inner voice are miracles of beauty and joy. . . . Any mistakes which may be made by a person who is obedient to the still small voice will be few, and they will not be sufficiently serious to be irretrievable; he can quickly pick himself up again and soon be wholly immersed in the Spirit. Mistakes are not fatal; not one is forever: Success is forever, but failure is only for a day.

If we make contact with the kingdom of God within us, we shall be living through God the rest of our days. Then spiritual sonship—God expressing Itself as individual Selfhood—will be revealed on earth. God formed us to manifest Itself on earth, to show forth Its glory, and that is our destiny. God planted His infinite abundance in the midst of us. Nothing need come to you or to me, but everything must flow out from us. And by what means? By that Presence, that Presence which heals, supplies, multiplies, and teaches. That Presence will perform every legitimate function of life, but It is only active in our life as we dedicate and consecrate ourselves to periods of meditation. Devotion and consecration are necessary to give us sufficient purpose so that we remember a dozen times a day to make no move without the realized Presence, or at least without an acknowledgment of It.[1]

As you study the principles of The Infinite Way, they become embedded and embodied within you—flesh of your flesh, blood of your blood, bone of your bone—and you will find then that when you sit down to do healing work or solely for communion with the Father, whereas, at first, you may call to mind a passage or two from Scripture to serve an inspirational purpose, very quickly, spontaneous truth, the daily manna, will begin to unfold to you from within yourself.

When you learn to live in this manner, you will find that you enter a new dimension of life, and a whole new experience opens up to you. If you begin to make a specific practice of meeting every hour of the day with a scriptural passage, eventually you will come to a place in consciousness where, instead of your remembering some passage, a new statement, or one you have known before, will come to you spontaneously from within. "He uttered his voice, the earth melted."[2] The moment the voice of God is uttered within you, whatever the particular earth of error, or discord, may be melts.

If you have a difficult day to face, perhaps even a little more difficult that you really can take care of, one that may tax you physically or financially more

[1] From the author's *Practicing the Presence* (New York: Harper & Brothers, 1958), pp. 105, 106, and (London: L. N. Fowler & Co. Ltd., 1956).

[2] Psalm 46:6.

than you can bear, or that may tax your understanding beyond your apparent spiritual development, instantly, if you have been abiding in the Word, a passage of Scripture comes into your thought:

> The Lord will perfect that which concerneth me.
>
> Psalm 138:8

> For he performeth the thing that is appointed for me.
>
> Job 23:14

> Greater is he that is in you, than he that is in the world.
>
> I John 4:4

You realize it is true that "the Father that dwelleth in me, he doeth the works.[1] . . . I can of mine own self do nothing"[2]—I am not expected to do anything of myself; it is the Father within me that lives my life for me, through me, and as me. With that realization, there comes a relaxing of tension, concern, fear, worry; and then the Father within can function normally through you. The word of God fills you with spiritual power: The word of God comes to you to perform your day's activity. The word of God goes before you to make straight the way. The word of God puts the right words in your mouth, if you need words; the right strength in your muscles, if you need muscles; and the right amount of money in your pocket, if you need money. The

[1] John 14:10. [2] John 5:30.

word of God does this as you learn to receive it within.

There may be other problems in the same day, the problem of health, perhaps, and then comes the remembrance:

> *God is life, infinite life; and therefore, God must be the life of man. That life which is God cannot be diseased. God, the life of man, cannot be weak; God, the life of man, cannot be old; God, the life of man, is infinite, immortal, and eternal.
>
> This is a truth that has been true since before the world began, and it has nothing to do with me or with my understanding. God is my life. How can I be worried? How can I be concerned about God's life? Certainly not about God's life! But I was thinking about my life. Is there any difference? Is there a God-life and a my-life? Is there a God-life and a your-life? Or is there only one infinite, eternal life, and is not that life God-life? Is that not your life and is it not my life?

The moment this becomes realized consciousness, a weight drops away, fear drops away; and you go about your business, the word of God having melted that particular "earth." But shortly thereafter, something else comes up in the day that to all appearances has more power than God. It may be a germ; it may be infection; it may be the report of a new and more devastating bomb or of a new epidemic sweeping the country, or it may be the unleashed fury of a hurricane speeding in your direction. It makes no difference what it is or what form it takes. The claim is that it is something more powerful than

God, but immediately the Word in which you have been abiding comes with a quick and sharp reminder:

> *God is one, one power. This thing, then, that is claiming to be power is not power: It is the "arm of flesh," or nothingness. Nothingness, nothingness! I know the world is afraid of this thing, but in the spiritual life, God alone is power—the Invisible alone is power.

Again that Spirit of God takes over and gives you peace.

Seek Only Spiritual Fruitage

"Choose you this day whom ye will serve."[1] In the world's state of material consciousness, the power of inertia will continue operating in individual consciousness until the finger of the Lord is upon one and then that person has no longer a choice as to whether or not he will remain in a material sense of life: He must turn to the spiritual path.

> Ye have not chosen me, but I have chosen you, and ordained you, that ye should go and bring forth fruit, and that your fruit should remain.
> John 15:16

God has already chosen you. You have already been touched by the finger of God and placed on the spiritual path. But even though God has placed you on that path and there is now no turning back, at this period of your unfoldment, there is still the

[1] Joshua 24:15.

opportunity for a choice: You can choose to let your progress be slow or to speed it up. You have the choice as to whether or not you will abide in the Word and so live with it that you are keeping your mind stayed on God constantly throughout the day and night, acknowledging God continuously: God as the source of your food, God as the source of your intelligence, God as the source of your spiritual strength, God as the infinity of your supply.

The more you practice this, the more you are opening your consciousness to the inflow of the Word, the voice of God, and when It utters Itself within you, the earth of error melts—the earth of material discords, the earth of material power—and you find yourself established in the spiritual life. However, if your mind is divided against itself, you will fail. If you are praying in the Spirit and through the Spirit and with the Spirit, but are thinking in terms of material good; if you are thinking of the fruitage of prayer as something you can see, hear, taste, touch, or smell, you will be postponing the day of your spiritual regeneration. When you pray, remember that God is Spirit, and pray only for the word of God and its spiritual fruitage.

Do not try to turn stones into bread; do not try to turn spiritual prayer into baker's bread or butcher's meat; do not pray to turn your spiritual communion with God into a material power of demonstration. Seek the kingdom of God, the word of God, and the fruitage of that Word. You will find that this Word translates itself of its own accord into the added things. Do not go to the Father for baker's bread, butcher's meat, farmer's vegetables, transportation, or currency, but let these be the added things. Your desire must always be for God and for His kingdom and His angels—spiritual fruitage—and, above all, that you may be receptive and responsive to the word of God which comes to you within your being as a still small voice.

Throughout the day and night, you will be tempted over and over again as was Jesus in the wilderness and later at Gethsemane. You will be tempted to fear some power, that is, you will be tempted to accept two powers. This belief in two powers may overwhelm you unless you have stabilized yourself in the principle of one power through continuous daily and hourly practice with each and every appearance. Whether it is in the newspaper, on the radio, or over television; whether it is in the experience of your family, your friends, or your relatives—every time that you are presented with something which testifies to two powers, you have to realize consciously:

> *There is no power external to my being, either for good or for evil. The kingdom of God, the kingdom of all Power is within me; and God-power is spiritual power. There is no power for good or for evil external to me. There is no power in thoughts or things: All power is in the word of God within me.

You will be confronted by untold dangers—not necessarily in your own personal life, but certainly in the lives of people around you—and you will have to stand alone in the midst of these dangers.

You will not be able to speak of what you have learned to anyone because no one would understand what you are saying, no one would be able to accept it. Only you, silently and secretly, will have to hold fast to your vision:

> *"Which of you convinceth me of sin?"[1] Who convinces me that there is a power besides God? Who convinces me that there is danger anywhere, or lack? God has given me dominion over everything in the air, the sky, the sea, and the earth, beneath the seas and beneath the earth. I shall not fear what man can do to me—physically or mentally. I shall not fear what mortal things can do to me—little things like germs or big things like bombs—because I recognize only one power, the word of God.

The fruits of this spiritual Word are harmony—physical, mental, moral, and financial harmony. The fruits of the word of God are life eternal. The word of God must be realized within you, and the fruitage of that Word will appear outwardly, visibly.

When a person arrives at that point of spiritual regeneration called illumination—the descent of the Holy Ghost or baptism of the Spirit—he has lost the capacity to sin. The human mind, that is, the mind that is unillumined with spiritual truth, always wants to benefit itself. It is not thinking in terms of the universal good, but it is usually thinking only of how it can benefit itself. Having recognized that the Spirit of the Lord is upon you, there is no longer

[1] John 8:46.

any reason to act in terms of what will be for your own benefit. When the Spirit of the Lord has been attained, there is complete freedom from all needs—physical, mental, moral, and financial. There is freedom, freedom in the Spirit, freedom in Christ, and there is no longer any bondage to the flesh, to sin, to disease, or to poverty.

The Word Can Only Be Revealed to the Selfless

No one can know the true word of God until he has come to a place in his spiritual unfoldment where never, under any circumstances, would he take advantage of this spiritual knowledge for personal gain, or misuse it in any way. When one has reached that stage of unfoldment, that pure state of consciousness, then it is that the true name of God is revealed. When that time comes, no longer do you worship a God in heaven; no longer do you look to a God for reward or do you fear a God of punishment. Now you know why Christ Jesus gave as his greatest revelation:

> *"I will never leave thee, nor forsake thee.[1] . . . I am with you alway, even unto the end of the world.[2] . . . I and my Father are one,"[3] and that Father is within me. *I* will always be with you. *I* in the midst of you am mighty.

When the sacred and secret name of God—the *I*—has been revealed to you, you have the Word. The fruitage of that Word is the grace of God—peace, joy, harmony, and abundance. With that sacred

[1] Hebrews 13:5. [2] Matthew 28:20. [3] John 10:30.

and secret Word in the forehead, you walk up and down this earth: You are seen as an ordinary man or woman, but your presence is felt as if you were a saint. You do not have to live by might or by power: You live solely by the Spirit of God which is now within you—by the word of God, by that secret Word, that sacred Word, that Word of power—not material or mental, but spiritual. The Word never has to be uttered because it continuously utters itself. You do not speak it; you hear it and you rest in its assurance.

As you walk up and down this earth, safe and secure in that Word, the fruitage appears outwardly as Scripture has promised. The fruitage of that Word is literally your food, your drink, your housing, and your clothing. It is your high tower. Yes, and God is the health of your countenance. You do not get health from God: God is your health. God is your safety and security; God is your peace. God never gives you anything: God is all things unto you. God, being infinite, cannot give you anything but Himself. Those who seek God for something other than the gift of Himself seek amiss and pray amiss. God is that which gives the gift of Himself as your life, your Soul, your spirit, your being, and even your body. Seek God! In finding God, you find rest, peace, harmony, joy—the fruits of the Spirit.

The life of God is the life of man. The Soul of God is the Soul of man. The Spirit of God is the Spirit of man. Even the body is the temple of the living God. And so it is that God, the Giver, appears on earth as God, the Gift—God, the Father; and God, the Son. There are not two; there is only one—God, the

Father, and God, the Son, always one, never two.

The word of God is within you, and that Word you know. Do not voice it as some do, but let it voice itself to you. Let it keep assuring you:

> **I* am ever with you. *I* will never leave you. If you go through the valley of the shadow of death, *I* will be with you. If you make your bed in hell, *I* will go with you. Whithersoever thou goest, *I* will go. *I* am come that you might have life, and that you might have it more abundantly.

The fruit of the Spirit is the fruit of the word of God held secretly, sacredly, and constantly within you.

Consciousness Unfolding

A review by A. S. Webb[1]

Joel Goldsmith's latest book, *Consciousness Unfolding,* will be read and appreciated by all metaphysical students. It is, as the name indicates, an explanation of processes of soul awakening and unfolding.

All the students who agree that man's problems stem from the fact that his personality has been dislocated, through detachment from his soul function, will know that his greatest need is soul awakening. Those of us who have reached that place in understanding will welcome this latest book of The Infinite Way writings for it discusses the processes of soul quickening and, under God's grace, the

[1] Reprinted from *The Seeker,* Perth, Western Australia, June, 1958.

unfolding of life when this new focus has been attained.

How to deal with appearances and the claims of the outer world of form, and to achieve inner conviction which comes from affinity with God are the main theme of this book which is obviously written for serious students and out of deep experience.

*   *   *

TRAVELOGUE

Our 1958 travel log covers approximately 50,000 miles, extending from Hawaii to Sydney, Melbourne, and Adelaide in the southeastern part of Australia, across the continent to Perth on the western coast; from Perth back again across to New Zealand; then to Hawaii by way of the Fiji Islands; across the Pacific to the mainland, stopping for lecture and class work in San Diego, Oklahoma City, Toledo, Indianapolis, Louisville, Chicago, and New York; from New York to London and Manchester, England, with a brief holiday in Scotland; from London to the Continent—Munich, Geneva, Amsterdam, and Zeist—and home.

In Holland, there is a group of influential people interested in the spiritual way of life, particularly in finding a means of bringing spiritual power into world affairs. These people hold a three day conference two or three times a year with guest speakers selected from around the globe. The most recent of these conferences was held in Zeist, Holland, August 29, 30, and 31, at which time there were two speakers from Germany, two from England, and it was my privilege to be the one invited from the United States.

There were some 250 people who had been invited to this conference because of their deep interest in the things of God which are "foolishness to man." These remarkable men and women are dedicated and consecrated to God and to the establishment of His reign on earth as it is in heaven. The association with all those in the conference was one of the most stimulating and soul-satisfying experiences of all my travels.

All those participating in the conference were lodged in one hotel, and the meetings were in a theatre in the same hotel. For three days, we lived in an atmosphere of religious devotion. After every meeting, there were discussion and question periods during which the invited guests were given the opportunity to ask questions of the speakers and discuss matters of a spiritual nature with them.

Our students realize, of course, what such a spiritually charged atmosphere does to all those assembled together and also to all the world which must feel its impulse. Emma and I were never for a moment released from that high consciousness, and it was while we were meditating together there that the message was given to us which changed all arrangements for this fall and sent me home to be quiet for these next few months. In a short time, a transcript of my talk to this group will be published in *The Letter*, and thereafter, from time to time, I will share more of this work with you.

Immediately after the final talk on Sunday morning, we had luncheon in Zeist, flew to London where we had dinner at the airport, flew out by the polar route of TWA at midnight, had breakfast about 20,000 feet over Labrador, a snack at the airport in Winnipeg, Canada—the only stop—luncheon in Los Angeles, and dinner in San Francisco.

Now home, home because of instructions to be quiet, home until further instructions, home for the holidays—Thanksgiving, Christmas, and the New Year.

What will the world find for which to give thanks this year? Many people will be grateful that the business recession seems to be fading and that the threatened danger of war in the Middle East seems to be easing. However, if we had one of the Hebrew prophets of gloom in our midst, he would probably remind us that the world economy will never be normal or good until the basic problem of wars and preparations for wars and the imbalance in world economy are corrected, and that peace will not be established on earth until trade relations comparable to those which exist among the forty-eight states of the Union are established among all the nations of the world. This seems a long way off.

For you individually, there may be many reasons for rejoicing and thanksgiving as the calendar year comes to a close. It might be wise for you to disregard the reasons others may have for thanksgiving and make this an occasion for a period of inner communion with God so that a real and good reason for gratitude may reveal itself to you.

For me, there is great rejoicing and gratitude this Thanksgiving Season because the major principles of The Infinite Way are being more broadly and more widely demonstrated than ever before; they are being understood and proved more conclusively than every before by students all over the world.

Throughout all ages the world has sought a greater power with which to overcome lesser powers. Always one power has been used to remove another, or the effects of another. The answer to this came to me when it was revealed that this eternal seeking for greater and greater powers to destroy larger and larger errors would never cease until the secret of *no-power* was learned. This is the Infinite Why:

> Not by might, nor by power, but by my spirit.
>
> Zechariah 4:6

> Be not afraid nor dismayed by reason of this great multitude; for the battle is not yours, but God's.
>
> Ye shall not need to fight in this battle: set yourselves, stand ye still, and see the salvation of the Lord with you.
>
> II Chronicles 20:15, 17

> Put up again thy sword into his place: for all they that take the sword shall perish with the sword.
>
> Matthew 26:52

> In returning and rest shall ye be saved; in quietness and in confidence shall be your strength.
>
> Isaiah 30:15

> Be strong and courageous, be not afraid nor dismayed for the king of Assyria, nor for all the

multitude that is with him: for there be more with us than with him:

With him is an arm of flesh; but with us is the Lord our God to help us.

II Chronicles 32:7, 8

I give thanks unto God who through His grace has revealed to me that "man shall not live by bread alone, but by every word that proceedeth out of the mouth of God."[1]

I give thanks that He has revealed to me a way of life by grace instead of by law.

I give thanks that God's grace has led to The Infinite Way the many students who are in a measure proving its principles.

I give thanks that God's grace has revealed these principles to human consciousness and that they are being published in the United States, in England, Holland, and Switzerland for all the world that has ears to hear and eyes to see.

[1] Matthew 4:4.

CHAPTER TWELVE: DECEMBER

THE ONE GREAT MIRACLE

SPOKEN or written words can never adequately convey the idea of the Christ. There is no way to understand the Christ except through the spiritual capacity of discernment—the Soul-capacities. Words are always inadequate.

In Hebrew Scripture, the term for the Christ is the Messiah. The Hebrews have always looked forward to the coming of a Messiah, but no one knows whether, in the beginning, they were expecting a man or whether they understood the term Messiah to mean a power or a presence. But whatever their concept of the Messiah, they knew Its function and what might be expected of It: The Messiah was to bring them freedom. That may be interpreted as political freedom since they were political slaves, or as economic freedom since they were in bondage to poverty, or as physical or moral freedom since there is no doubt but that they were slaves to sensuality and to the characteristics that were bred in the conditions in which they found themselves. It may be that they thought of the Messiah as freeing them from outside influences, or they may have understood the word more correctly than we imagine: They may have understood the Messiah to be that which freed them from themselves—from their slavery to sense, their slavery to false ideas, their slavery to ignorance.

To me, the Messiah is that which frees us from ourselves, from a limited sense of self. We are never enslaved by anybody or any condition, except by that which we have either made or accepted for ourselves. We make our own conditions of slavery or we passively accept conditions without a realization that there is that within us which could set us free.

The Hebrews, however, did come to a place where their expectancy was a man. Isaiah speaks of that man as the Prince of Peace, the mighty Counsellor, one whose name shall be called Wonderful. To a man of such enlightenment as Isaiah, it may be that although using the term, "man" or "he", he really was referring to a spiritual Presence, a Power, that which permeates all being, that which is never seen in and of itself, but which is always seen and heard by Its effect. The Messiah means God with us, the presence of God, the Spirit of God. But when it is translated into the Greek language, the Messiah becomes the Christ—the Messiah in Hebrew and Aramaic, the Christ in Greek.

The Message and the Messenger Become One

To bring this Christ, the Messiah or Spirit of God, to our consciousness, let us for a moment accept the fact that It is not a man, but that It is some kind of a spiritual impulse, presence, or power, which appears or acts through man, which acts *as* man. That is the reason the Christ cannot be separated from the man, Jesus, because they became *one.* There is no way to separate a message from a messenger because they become one. The message, however, is always greater than the messenger. In time, every messenger disappears from visible sight, but the message remains and is carried on by others. If you understand this, you will never be confused and misled into worshipping a man or a woman. You know that the Christ can never disappear as long as there is an individual on earth through whom It may appear, and when there are no men or women or children on earth, you need not be surprised if It should come through a rock.

To some, it is absolutely essential that the Christ appear through the medium of words or thought, and so it is necessary for the Christ to translate Itself to some people as thoughts, and to others, It must be conveyed through the medium of speech. There are a few, however, for whom no process is necessary—no thoughts, no words. These few could sit in the silence in a state of receptivity, thinking no thoughts whatsoever, and they would receive a message. The Christ unites us and makes a bond between us which requires no words, no thoughts, and yet there is an understanding that takes place between us—the glint of an eye, the touch of a finger. It is something very sacred and very holy. There are students in this work who have experienced it so often that they understand it thoroughly.

All of us must eventually come to that place where we do not "trust in chariots, because they are many; and in horsemen, because they are very strong,"[1] where we do not look to "man, whose breath is in his nostrils,"[2] not even to his thoughts. We do not look

[1] Isaiah 31:1. [2] Isaiah 2:22.

to human strength—physical strength or mental power; we do not look to anything that is in the realm of the creature, that is, to anything which is already made, but look only to the Holy One of Israel, the Infinite Invisible.

To human beings, that seems very intangible, ephemeral, and vague, but it must become less so until that very Invisible becomes the visible and tangible. The Christ, or the Messiah, is that presence, power, and influence, which is within all of us, but which is not available to us until demonstrated: The Christ is in the saint and in the sinner; the Christ is in the sick man and in the well man; the Christ is in the consciousness of the rich and the poor, the white, the black, and the yellow, because the Christ is omnipresence, known to the Chinese as Tao, to the Hindus as Brahm, to the Hebrews as Emmanuel, or Messiah, to the Christians as the Christ, but always one and the same thing—the presence of God with us.

Healing Is the Sign of the Miracle

The Christ, although It is ever present, is not available to the worldly man until that man has risen above dependence on that which is visible or tangible to human sense and has learned the meaning of the transcendental, that which is invisible to sight, inaudible to hearing, and yet real, strong, and powerful. Our work is the opening of consciousness to the Christ. As the Christ is realized, we find ourselves coming into greater harmony of mind, body, business, purse, and home. We, likewise, find that we are able, even as the Master and the disciples were, to bring a measure of that healing to all those who are receptive and responsive to It—not to all people, however, because there are those who seek only loaves and fishes, only better physicality, and although some of them are healed, we do not accomplish our best work with them.

Healing is of paramount importance in the work of The Infinite Way because, although healing is not the object of our work, healing is the sign that follows the realization and demonstration of the Christ. As you, through study, reading, prayer, meditation, and communion with God, bring yourself to a state of consciousness in which the Christ becomes a reality—becomes tangible—you will find that the Christ takes over your life, literally going before you to make the crooked places straight, literally walking beside you, invisible yet so tangible that you know this Presence is with you and you feel Its effects in your life.

It is this Power, recognized and realized, which does the healing work: Healing work is not accomplished by knowing the truth, but knowing the truth is a preparation leading to healing, leading to that state of consciousness in which we become receptive to the Christ. The healing work, however, is only accomplished in that split second when the Christ is made evident, when that feeling of awareness or release takes place within us.

The Infinite Way form of healing does not involve telling the patient to be other than he is, that is, it does not involve telling him to be more loving or more just, or more moral or more anything. It takes him right where he is, accepts him as he is, and permits this Christ to enter his consciousness and do the transforming rather than making the healing contingent on the patient's efforts to be a better human being. There is nothing wrong with making an effort humanly to be better, and we are always doing that to some extent, but no amount of human effort to make one's self better will transform a person's life. To bring this about, this greater Power, the Christ, must find entrance into consciousness. Then, and then only, does the transformation take place.

Devotion Is Requisite

Saul of Tarsus was a very good man, a man who spent his days and nights pondering God, deeply religious, believing in God, fearing for God's kingdom so much that he was willing to do almost anything to protect his God and his God's way of life. His was such an intense passion for God that he would permit nothing to stand in the way of his achieving the realization of God. In the midst of his zeal, the realization came: He was struck blind with a tremendous power of light, and, then, he who had persecuted the Christians became one of the great apostles of Christianity. All the years that he had spent learning about an unknown God, a God "whom therefore ye ignorantly worship"[1] as he later termed it—all the years of zealous, almost fanatical, devotion to God were profitable to him.

And so it is with us: Every affirmation we have ever made, every denial we have ever made, every right thought we have ever entertained, or every attempt we have made humanly to improve ourselves

[1] Acts 17:23.

is a help along the way. If we persist in it with enough devotion, we shall come to that place where we, too, are struck with the light of Truth, and, in that blinding flash, we shall know that the Christ exists as a living reality. The Christ is not right thinking; the Christ is not knowledge of truth; and the Christ is not a book about truth: The Christ is an actual, living reality that no one yet has ever been able to explain, but which ever so many people have been able to entertain within themselves and to experience.

When we no longer have faith in "the horses and horsemen of Egypt," when we no longer have faith in swords or material remedies or thoughts or anything that is in the visible or tangible world, we come to a moment when we have nothing to cling to: It is that moment when we cry out in desperation, as did Mary, "They have taken away my Lord."[1] That is the day! That is the moment of glory, the moment when we have no Lord—nothing to cling to, not a thought to hold on to, not a belief. Nothing in which we have had faith remains. That is the most glorious moment of our whole career because when every tangible "horse and horseman" have been taken away from us, when all our guns and bombs have been taken away and all these "right thoughts" have failed and we have nothing left, no *thing* left, that is when we have the Christ. That is when the Spirit takes over and says, "Have you forgotten *Me*? *I* am still with you. If you go through the waters, you will not drown; if you go through the flames, they will not kindle upon you. *I* will never leave you

[1] John 20:13.

nor forsake you. Before Abraham was, *I* am. *I* will be with you until the end of the world."

And we turn around and say, "I forgot all about *I*. I was looking for a thought; I was looking for a statement of truth; I was looking for a good practitioner; I was looking for a new teaching."

"Yes, *I* know you were, and *I* was standing back here—*I*, always *I*. *I* in the midst of you am mighty. *I* am the Lord God of Israel, the very Christ, or Son of God, in you."

"Yes, *I* in the midst of me is mighty. Paul saw ('a man in Christ . . . whether in the body . . . or whether out of the body, I cannot tell')[1]—whether in physical form or not I know not, but I saw that Creature. I do not even know if it was externalized; it may have been within my own being."

"And it was, because *I* never get outside of you. *I* never become external to you. *I* am always in the midst of you. *I* is the very consciousness of your own being. *I* is your Soul; *I* is the very bread and meat and wine. *I* in the midst of thee *Is*. *I* has meat the world knows not of. *I* can give you water, living water. *I* is the bread of life."

Just think of that: *I* is that—and we have been looking in a book for it; we have been looking to a man for it; we have been looking to some teaching for it. The Hebrews of old made the mistake of thinking that the Messiah would be a man instead of realizing that the Messiah would come in the form of a man, as a messenger bringing them the awareness of the Christ. After Jesus' time, it was thirty years before the Christ-light came to Paul, and it was

[1] II Corinthians 12:2.

ninety years after the Master was no longer visible on the earth before John of Patmos, the greatest exponent of the Christ, the greatest witness of the Christ of whom we have any knowledge, had the vision of the Christ. This experience could come to them only because the Christ, *I*, is ever present, omnipresent.

I was omnipresent in Paul; *I* was omnipresent in John; and *I* is omnipresent in every saint and sinner on earth, awaiting first the acknowledgment of It, and then the recognition of It. We become aware of the Christ in proportion to the moments of receptive silence we experience. No person who does not set aside enough time, both day and night, even though that time may be divided into periods of only two or three minutes each, will become receptive and responsive to the Christ—unless it is in a period of terrible danger. I hope that none of us will have to wait until we are in a dungeon somewhere, or at death's door before we open ourselves to the Christ.

We have the same opportunity of having It revealed within us as anyone else has. You may say that someone else has more leisure. You might even say that I had more leisure. But I did not find the Christ in my leisure. When I was in the business world out on the road selling merchandise or making trips to Europe to buy merchandise, I had to take time for reading and introspection. I was busy, as busy as any of you are, but I had to learn to put first things first. That is the lesson we all have to learn. We always find time to do the things we really want to do. If there is a sufficient God-hunger within you, you, too, will find the necessary time in which to pray to God to be shown the way, and a highway will open before you.

You will find that with these frequent periods of meditation, with enough practice, eventually it will happen: One of those flash seconds will come as it did to Paul, probably in a lesser degree, possibly in a greater degree, because there is no limit except the limit of our receptivity. It will happen! And when it happens, you will know what I mean when I say the Christ is our salvation, the Christ is our health, the Christ is our supply, and the Christ is our guidance, direction, and protection. The Christ is all in all to us as the Christ is realized.

The Christ Is the Miracle

Those who have experienced the Christ already know that it is a miracle-experience and that it results in miracles. Many people, even in our work, do not believe in miracles. They cannot accept miracles as a possibility or a fact. How many of you, who have been in metaphysics for the past ten, fifteen, or twenty years have ever counted up how few days you have been sick or how many times you have been quickly healed without surgery, without medicine, and, furthermore, without the financial burden frequent medical care entails. If that is not a miracle in and of itself, what is it? How many of your children have avoided many of the children's diseases? If you will remember the degree of immunity you have experienced in these and other areas, you will know that miracles are happening to you every day. If a simple headache is healed, that in and of itself is a miracle. Why? Because it was done by Something that no one in the world has ever been able to explain. Every time the slightest ill is healed spiritually, you have witnessed the presence of God, the activity of the Christ. That is the miracle.

The healing is not the miracle: The fact that we have experienced the activity of the Christ is the miracle. We have thought that the opening of the Red Sea was the miracle; we have thought that the multiplying of the loaves and fishes was the miracle. No, that was the effect of the miracle: The miracle was the omnipresence of the Christ; the miracle was witnessing the activity of the Christ which resulted in multiplied loaves and fishes or in healing. *The miracle is the experience of the Christ.* What happens in human experience is the result of the miracle. Do not look for the results of the miracle until you have experienced the miracle itself—the miracle of the experience of the Christ!

That is why so many people miss the miracle: They think that a healing is a miracle. Spiritual healing cannot take place without the activity of the Christ. The Christ is the miracle; the healing is an inevitability. Everything that happens after the experience of the Christ is an inevitability—greater health, greater wealth, greater safety, greater security, greater everything. The miracle is the demonstration and experience of the Christ. When you have experienced that, you will witness a miracle such as nobody in the world will believe except those who have experienced it.

Those early Christians who were in prison and had their manacles stricken off experienced the Christ:

It was the Christ, an invisible Nothingness, that broke the manacles. That was the miracle—the Invisibility that did it! Daniel in the lion's den—is that a miracle? No, but what shut the lion's mouth is the miracle. Once the lion's mouth is shut, there is nothing miraculous about Daniel's standing there. You and I would stand there, too, if we had something with which to shut the lion's mouth. Who is afraid of lions when their mouths are shut?

Do you see what the miracle is? The miracle is the Christ. All the rest is the effect of that one great miracle. Never be concerned about a demonstration. Never look for a sign. Never look for an outer symbol. Be concerned about one thing only—experiencing the Christ. Make room in your consciousness for the inflow, because when it comes, you will be able to say with Paul, "I live; yet not I, but Christ liveth"[1] my life. Christ is the way; Christ is the truth; Christ is the medicine; Christ is the bread; Christ is the wine; Christ is the water.

Let us demonstrate the Christ on earth, and we shall have peace on earth. But do not try to have the miracle of peace on earth without the Christ because it cannot happen. Do not expect any kind of peace between individuals; do not even expect to find peace within yourself. You could be all alone on a barren island and yet be in torture. But if you have the Christ, you will be at peace. Except the Christ be born in us, there is no peace.

Our faith must be in the Christ, not in any man or woman, not in anything external to us. Our faith must be in the Invisible. Our faith may at first be in

[1] Galatians 2:20.

the invisible Christ of Jesus, Isaiah, John, or anybody who shows forth evidences of the presence of the Christ. These great spiritual lights are the way-showers, but in the end we must come back to the Christ of our own being: *I*, Itself, is the way: "*I* am the way, the truth, and the life."[1] *I* is that—the *I* of you and the *I* of me.

ACROSS THE DESK

Christmas offers a special opportunity to give gifts as an outer expression of an inner love and gratitude. This I do enjoy, but most of all I treasure the association of the season with the life, message, and mission of Christ Jesus. During this period I spend many hours of the day and night in meditation and often "feel" the presence of the Teacher of Nazareth.

Miracles are taking place in the world today—and the world knoweth it not. The grace of God has sent men and women to earth in all ages to show the world the miracle of grace. Travel the world wherever you may—today the earth is filled with His glory. His presence shines in the faces of men and women in every land, so that the longed for day of spiritual freedom cannot be far away.

Newspapers report only the dark clouds of sense moving in front of the heavenly bodies. Good is seldom news. To behold Him walking the earth, striding the skies, filling the minds and bodies of men, it is necessary to open the inner eye and the inner ear and see what is going on behind the scenes.

On one of my recent trips I met a woman to whom

[1] John 14:6.

people come in such thousands that she can give each one but two minutes, and yet blessings and healings flow like sand through a sieve. The miracle is not only the woman—and a miracle she truly is—but the miracle is that thousands in the world are so spiritually attuned as to find her. I met a man so God-inspired that thousands disobeyed the orders of their church to flock to him to receive God's grace as it flowed through him, and ministers disobeyed their superiors to open the church doors that had been closed to let him minister to the sick, the hungry, the empty.

Never perhaps in all history have so many doctors, psychologists, and psychiatrists come to the spiritual centers of the world seeking for that bread which cometh down from heaven. Never perhaps have so many government officials been willing to listen and to read about the Power which is not a power *over* anything or anybody, but which is just the power of grace.

The miracle itself is that so many are turning from the dead letter of ceremony and ritual to seek the living waters which constantly flow forth from the Souls of the illumined. As the holy men of the East are honored, respected, and revered, so today I see the miracle of recognition being given to the illumined of the West.

All of us need to lose the pride of intellect which denies miracles and becomes childlike enough to behold the miracles which fill the earth at this very moment—not only the miracles of mechanical achievement, miraculous as they are, but also the great miracle, the miracle of God's grace restoring sick minds and bodies and raising up men filled with spiritual vision to create a new type of government.

Spiritual healing results not so much because of what you *know* as because of what you *feel*. It is the letting go of mental striving and struggling and letting God's grace reveal itself. The greatest miracle in heaven or on earth is God's grace. Spiritual healing comes "not by might, nor by power",[1] but by God's grace; spiritual wisdom unfolds not "by taking thought,"[2] but by the realization of His presence. "Ye shall not need to fight"[3] for "where the Spirit of the Lord is, there is liberty."[4] In God's presence is fullness of life.

In this *Letter* you have read the miracle of my life —the experience of the Christ revealing Itself as a living Presence. Here you read how the consciousness of this Presence becomes the new dimension of life, Christ, and how It appears as our daily good. The great joy in all this is that the Experience came to me when I was living the normal human life of a businessman with most of its human faults and little of its virtues, although it undoubtedly came because of the depth of my longing to know God.

The greater joy came later when I realized that all men may experience God, if so be they truly seek Him rather than seek that which may come through Him. This is the secret. Ponder this all through the holiday season when His spirit is hovering close to the world and ready for entrance—if we but bid Him enter.

[1] Zechariah 4:6.
[2] Matthew 6:27.
[3] II Chronicles 20:17.
[4] II Corinthians 3:17.

I cannot see December roll by without telling you of the deep love and the heart full of gratitude for all of you who constitute my household. But you do understand, I know.

P.O. Box 5308,
Honolulu,
Hawaii.